The Story of Creation in the Qur'an
– A Sufi Interpretation –

Shaykh Fadhlalla Haeri

Distributed & Published by Zahra Publications
PO Box 50764
Wierda Park 0149
Centurion
South Africa
E-mail: info@askonline.co.za
www.zahrapublications.com
www.askonline.co.za

© 2013 Shaykh Fadhlalla Haeri

All rights reserved. Except for brief quotations in critical articles or reviews, no part of this book may be reproduced or utilised in any form or by any means, electronic or mechanical, without permission in writing from the publisher.

Designed and typeset in South Africa by Adli Jacobs

To Purchase an eBook version of this book, please visit the eBook portal on www.askonline.co.za

Printed and bound in South Africa by Ultra Litho Printers (Pty) Ltd

ISBN 978--1-919826-73-8

The Story of Creation in the Qur'an
– A Sufi Interpretation –

Shaykh Fadhlalla Haeri

Zahra Publications

Contents

Preface vii

Introduction xi

1: Emergence of the Universe 1

2: Life on Earth and its Diversity 21

3: Humanity and its Journey 37

4: Wisdom, God-Consciousness and Revelations 65

5: End of Life and the Universe 83

Glossary 99

ties, logic and reason. It connects humanity with its essence in Divine Reality. Accordingly, Qur'anic science deals with the inimitability of the Qur'an, thereby all exegesis or commentary look at the historical context in which a verses is revealed, its grammar, eloquence, traditional pronunciation and the method in which it is read.

The Qur'an contains the blueprint of existence as well as the perfect manner of transaction with oneself, nature, society, and the Creator. The Qur'an is like a universal divine mirror that reflects whatever there is in the universe in a manner that can be understood and adhered to by any human being who seeks transformation and awakening to the everlasting source and essence that lies within the heart (consciousness). Much depends upon our intention; faith and a courteous approach to the sacred text are paramount for wherever we then look there are signs of the Creator, signs that we can only see due to His grace and generosity.

Furthermore, the Qur'an reveals patterns and maps of the universe, known and unknown. It shines the Truth upon what is in the heavens and on the earth, connecting the physical with unseen energies and realities; it draws similitudes, parables or metaphors to a web of patterns that connect based on the one field that pulsates throughout the universe. It establishes that human reason is an essential starting point that leads to subtler understanding, insight, and higher consciousness.

In addition, we often see in the Qur'an a recurrence of similar themes, which is like the emergence of a pattern in a mosaic, or threads in a tapestry, where the use of the same tile patterns complements another pattern and holds the total design together. We see a multifaceted panorama dealing with various aspects of existence in multi-dimensions of form and meanings that take the reader to higher levels of consciousness towards a unified and integrated view of existence. This hierarchy of patterned style is also utilised by the author in this book in order to aid the reader in his journey of ascension.

The physical realm that is accessible to our senses and its scientific and technological extensions are forms that inevitably veil the intrinsic nature or essence of existence. Every form hides a meaning and contains the essence, the spirit that emanates from Allah. Thus, our earthly world can only ever be indicative of the subtler Reality that becomes evident in the hereafter, once all the veils have been extinguished.

Moreover, the Qur'an reveals the intricate connections in the fabric of reality and the levels of causality. In our daily lives, every event or

Preface

Say: Journey in the land, then behold how He originated creation; then Allah causes the later growth to grow; Allah is powerful over everything. [29:20]

The Qur'an is a sacred source book, a guidance through the landscape of personal consciousness towards our origins in the everlasting abode of absolute pure consciousness.

"The Story of Creation" is an exposition of the Qur'anic verses relating to the nature of physical phenomena, including the origins of the universe, the nature of light, matter, space and time, and the evolution of biological and sentient beings. In this book Shaykh Fadhlalla Haeri demonstrates that the verses in the Qur'an relating to the outer physical phenomena are not separate from inner phenomena and states, but in fact reflect them. The Qur'an gives us a unified view of existence drawing us from multiplicity to unity, in order to live appropriately from a unified foundation in a world of multiplicity. This is missing from other books, which only focus on matching outer phenomena to scientific discovery without inner reflection. The Story of Creation relates outer patterns and symbols to inner experiences and metaphors bringing out the gnostic elements not just the prescriptive and phenomenal descriptions.

For Muslims, the gateway to spiritual knowledge is the Qur'an, which itself is the verbal expression of ultimate reality, the all-comprehensive speech of Allah. Accordingly the root meaning of the word Qur'an also means gathered or all-comprehensive. The Qur'an was thereby revealed to the all-comprehensive Adamic consciousness (heart) of the Prophet Muhammad (pbuh).

The Qur'an has also been referred to as the Book, the Light, the Balance, the Discrimination, the Guidance, and the Remembrance among others. The Qur'an's power is due to its consistency regarding the Truth that all of creation is held by God's unique cosmic will and Oneness; and to its description of the patterns of creation, and the appropriate code of conduct by employing parables, historical stories and wise guidelines for personal and social wellbeing. The special language of the Qur'an bridges the gap between the unseen realm and the world of physical enti-

experience we encounter presents a challenge from which we may grow in personal or spiritual wisdom. The universe is like a womb woven by space and time, containing countless interacting entities, each bounded by birth and death, and restricted by conditioned mental and cultural limitations. Discernment and discrimination come about whenever reason and causality take place within the confines of space and time, which in itself is a transient reality that floats in infinite timelessness. Humanity's earthly perch is a conditioned aspect of universal realities.

The Qur'an emphasizes the basic patterns that govern earthly physical realities and connects them to their heavenly root, to which all return. It illustrates the relativity of time and space so that we may see our earthly concerns in the proper perspective through the referral to timeless qualities. Through God-consciousness, all other misunderstandings stabilize appropriately.

All of the entities of existence, including stars and galaxies are described as being held together by Allah's will, up to an appointed time, after which they will disintegrate and return to the original singularity or 'no-thingness,' that originally gave rise to 'everything-ness'. The beginning of creation is described as a singular occurrence like a crack in the unseen. From an absolute singularity with infinite possibility emerged a spectrum of diverse and expanding entities, which will eventually return to the point of the original state of no-thingness.

Further, the Qur'an stipulates that creation always appears in pairs and as complementary opposites. Every entity in existence is balanced and rooted in its apparent opposite; every 'negative' is connected to a 'positive'. Allah's decrees do not change, but individual and societal destinies change according to the paths followed. Human beings are guided to Truth and Light according to the extent of their individual readiness and ability to be transformed. The One Source behind all actions and attributes can be realized only by transcending all dualities and causalities. To see the one essence at the root of every situation implies seeing total perfection in the moment. This happens when all 'otherness' fades away under the light of 'Oneness'.

Reality, therefore, is a reflection of the divine attributes, which are the names of Allah. He is the absolute Truth which manifests in infinitely myriad ways and to different extents in creation and human experience. Allah is the only truth, and every other entity is a minor reflection of this absolute state. "The Story of Creation in the Qur'an" emphasizes the way in which the Qur'an itself is a verbal revelation of truth through the reality of the perfected prophetic consciousness.

Faith and trust in the all-merciful God are required for proper understanding and absorption of the message of the Qur'anic revelation. This book of treasures will only impact upon those whose hearts are ready to be illumined. The light of the Qur'an is barred from the sceptics and those in denial of their own essence and of the One all comprehensive reality – Allah. "The Story of Creation in the Qur'an" brings the Book of Treasures one step closer to those whose hearts are ready to be illumined.

Dr. Adnan al-Adnani

Introduction

The Qur'an is the principal source book upon which Islam is based. The Qur'an describes the creation of heavens and earth and their development and progress over a period of time, giving graphic descriptions of the collapse of the earth, stars, and the whole of the universe as we know it – back to its origin of 'no-thingness'.

Furthermore, the Qur'an tells us about the metaphysical, universal and specific aspects of creation, giving special attention to human life, along with descriptions and prescriptions for wholesome living. The Noble Qur'an is full of signs, allegories, metaphors and historical events which illustrate the appropriate way of conduct that enhances natural stability, harmony, happiness, knowledge of God and His way. Thus it also describes the different stages and states which human beings go through before and after death. A considerable portion of the Qur'an is devoted to life after death and how to prepare for it in this life. Indeed, life on earth is considered a prelude to and preparation for what will be experienced after death.

The entire creation of the universe began by a mysterious instantaneous event which is often referred to as the Divine Command: "Be!" After several billion years life on earth began after a long period of cosmic rain which caused life to emerge from a 'dead' earth. Then came the rest of creation and the eventual rise of consciousness, awareness and, ultimately, the emergence of the Adamic being who is both heavenly and earthly in composition. Because of this potential of consciousness, human beings are held as stewards over the rest of creation by virtue of their mental capacity as well as their evolved soul or spirit at heart.

There are considerable similarities between the Qur'an's description of creation and the story from the Bible (Genesis 1, King James version):

1   *In the beginning God created the heaven and the earth.*
2   *And the earth was without form, and void; and darkness was upon the face of the deep. And the Spirit of God moved upon the face of the waters.*
3   *And God said, Let there be light: and there was light.*
4   *And God saw the light, that it was good: and God divided the*

light from the darkness.

5 *And God called the light Day, and the darkness he called Night. And the evening and the morning were the first day.*
6 *And God said, Let there be a firmament in the midst of the waters, and let it divide the waters from the waters.*
7 *And God made the firmament, and divided the waters which were under the firmament from the waters which were above the firmament: and it was so.*
8 *And God called the firmament Heaven. And the evening and the morning were the second day....*
9 *And God said, Let the waters under the heaven be gathered together unto one place, and let the dry land appear: and it was so.*
10 *And God called the dry land Earth; and the gathering together of the waters called the Seas: and God saw that it was good.*
11 *And God said, Let the earth bring forth grass, the herb yielding seed, and the fruit tree yielding fruit after his kind, whose seed is in itself, upon the earth: and it was so...*
13 *And the evening and the morning were the third day.*
14 *And God said, Let there be lights in the firmament of the heaven to divide the day from the night; and let them be for signs, and for seasons, and for days, and years...*
29 *And God said, Behold, I have given you every herb bearing seed, which is upon the face of all the earth, and every tree, in which is the fruit of a tree yielding seed; to you it shall be for meat.*
30 *And to every beast of the earth, and to every fowl of the air, and to everything that creepeth upon the earth, wherein there is life, I have given every green herb for meat: and it was so.*
31 *And God saw everything that he had made, and, behold, it was very good. And the evening and the morning were the sixth day.*

Many of the stories told in the Qur'an have their equivalent in the Bible with some variation. The Arabs of Makkah often interacted with Christian and Jewish merchants and country folks. As a result many of the old Abrahamic ideas about creation were not unfamiliar to the Arabs. As time went by each of the ancient apostles tried to explain the story of creation to their peoples in language that could be understood at that time.

The metaphor of the rise and descent of Adam is described as God's will to create a worthy steward on earth who could know all the divine attributes and qualities of God and thus behave with compassion and grace (*khalifah*). The Adamic consciousness rose in 'Paradise', where everything was perfect and not subject to change or decay. Then Adam was made to 'descend' to earth in order to be exposed to the dynamic of life, dualities, numerous creations and transient realities. God graced Adam with a divine soul which knows Allah's desirable qualities and is the direct link to Him.

Human beings on earth are in a constant state of struggle; they are driven to understand the soul and the divine Presence that pervades the Universe. Man on earth is regarded as the 'Khalifah', the steward or divine representative in relation to other creations. The Qur'an regards human responsibility as being comprehensive regarding life on earth. It warns against egotistic tendencies, waste or injustices at all levels. Social life and communities are regarded as essential for human development and spiritual awakening. Dualities and multiplicities are seen as emanating from Oneness and returning to it. The enlightened human being regards a potential enemy as a friend. 'Otherness' is seen through the light of Oneness. This does not preclude common folk from judging or condemning other people and situations according to their values and actions.

The Qur'an mentions numerous other creations that exist in different realms, but only a few of them are known to us. These include Angels, Jinn and other entities and subtle forces that regulate the universe. The Qur'an also describes other creations as more powerful than what we experience on earth.

Life on earth is based on dualities and pluralities which can appear either in opposition or in complementarity. Human life and experiences are described as a sample of what is much richer in the hereafter. Lives are framed within specific periods of time and limited space. We experience perpetual challenges which can either lead to a better understanding of the unifying forces leading to unity or to confusion and disappointment. The path of Islam – living the Qur'an and the Prophetic way – gives guidelines to reconciliation with the world as is and the understanding of creation at large, as well as inner states of mind and heart. The enlightened person realises that change and diversity are veils to ever-present constancy and Unity – Allah.

Human beings always seek wellbeing and happiness. That state is the result of a harmonious relationship between the changing self and the constant soul or spirit. The human quest is mostly to changes in time and space and is a mysterious presence.

The beginning of creation occurred like a crack in the unseen, or 'no-thingness,' giving rise to 'everythingness'. From an intensely dense and absolute singularity emerged infinite diversity and expanding entities, which will eventually return to the point of original emergence or singularity. The Qur'an describes this process as: "The same way it began it will return". The universe is held together by divine power described as 'Light'.

The purpose and meaning of humanity is to perfect the knowledge of Allah's attributes and qualities by means of transformative worship. This knowledge, trust, and guiding light will lead to success, contentment in this life and the hereafter. The so-called 'descent of Adam to earth' is the driving force for the conscious and deliberate ascent back to the state of the eternal garden or Paradise (within the heart on earth, before the hereafter). The Qur'an gives detailed prescriptions for this process which is founded upon doing good (selfless service and transcendence of ego) and improving intention, attention and action. The light of Allah and His will permeates the whole universe, governs it and guides it to its destiny in ways that are discernible as well as unseen and unknowable.

The mysterious inception of creation of the universe occurs within the boundaries of space and time. Our universe, and maybe other universes, are defined by such parameters and limits. On earth we clearly experience the arrow of time which moves from the past to the future via the present. Whatever is born or created is on its way towards its end or death. Order and disorder mingle intimately in the ocean of energy fields and space. At the point of inception of creation there was perfect order in that absolute Oneness. Astronomers estimate that the earth and the solar system began about 4.5 billion years ago and we are now nearly half way towards their end. Every entity or energy moves between its original gathered state (Oneness) and subsequent dispersion and separation, after which it returns to its original state.

Progress in science and technology has enabled us to understand better the creational dynamics, boundaries and connectedness of systems, large and small. We are, however, reaching a point where a great deal of effort and resources yield less and less helpful information. We seem to be nearing the boundaries where the discernible and unknowable meet. This is where normal human intellect and consciousness need to yield to higher consciousness and the realm of spiritual insight and imagination.

In this book I have restricted myself to expounding upon verses in the Qur'an that describe different aspects of our universe and only occasionally do I refer to our modern day knowledge regarding astronomy and quantum mechanics. As a young scientist I had been amazed by Qur'anic revelations fusing limited consciousness with the supreme Reality. My respect, love and trust in the Qur'an had been my guiding principle towards a better understanding of life and especially that of human nature. This gift has been the driving force behind producing this book for the general reader. Each human being is a microcosm that reflects the macrocosm and this reality is the greatest gift for us humans. Our purpose in life is to realise and experience this great truth and gift.

Until a few decades ago science considered particles and fields to be distinct entities. Then came Quantum Theory and its unified view which brought an end to the dualism of matter and energy. The revolutionary idea that there is no separate or independent material reality brought about a considerable shift in our viewpoints in science, as well as in philosophy and religion. Empty space consists of particles and antiparticles being spontaneously created and annihilated. This mysterious suspension is the origin of everything that exists and that can exist. This 'nothing' of space is the womb of the universe. We human beings are within that womb and (mysteriously) contain that womb within us. The large space between the nucleus of the atom and an orbiting electron is considered as empty space and it is there that all 'virtual effects' take place. This is the foundation of our so-called real world; a virtual reality that's ever-changing and is based on inherent uncertainty. The Real is ever constant and is the source of all that is known and unknown. In Truth there is only the Real.

Timeline of Creation

According to present day scientific discoveries

Big Bang
13.7 billion years ago – Emergence of the universal and cosmic background radiation. Numerous thresholds where chemistry and physics both at the nuclear level and at the visible levels take place.

12 billion years ago – Stars and galaxies.

4.6 billion years ago – Solar system emerges.

3.8 billion years ago – Life on earth and increased level of oxygen.

600 million years ago – After millions of years of a sterile period, bacteria appear along tidal pools leading to multi-cellular organisms. Most prominent is the jelly fish which is without basic sensation and motor response.

500 million years ago – First vertebrates with forebrain, mid- and hindbrain appear.

400 million years ago – Sharks and amphibians appear.

300 million years ago – Reptiles and winged insects with traces of social organization appear.

300 million years ago – Pangaea is formed = Supercontinent.

250 million years ago – Mammals and dinosaurs appear.

200 million years ago – First birds (well-developed visual system) appear.

150 million years ago – First flowering plants appear.

100 million years ago – India breaks away from Antarctica.

60 million years ago – North America splits from Europe. Atlantic Ocean is born.

45 million years ago – India collides with Eurasia and Himalayas rise from the ocean.

INTRODUCTION

25 million years ago – Grass and herbivores appear.

20 million years ago – Apes and Monkeys separate.

7 million years ago – Hominids and early bi-pedals appear, then Homo Habilis, Homo Erectus and others, such as Neanderthals.

7 million years ago – Chimpanzee and Hominids separate. Improved tools and empathy.

2 million years ago – Homo Habilis with double brain size appears.

500,000 years ago – Complex tools and increased brain size develop.

150,000 years ago – Homo Sapiens appear, with agricultural instruments, innovations in speech, skills and teaching (the earliest skeletal remains of modern humans are dated 160,000 years ago, or earlier, with a brain capacity three times that of early Hominids).

120,000 years ago – Evidence emerges of burial rituals (afterlife) and recognition of 'heavenly power'.

70,000 years ago – Migration out of Africa.

10,000 years ago – Agriculture.

6,000 years ago – Writing.

5,000 years ago – Civilizations.

600 years ago – Printing press.

200 years ago – Industrial Revolution.

50 years ago and today – Computers, Laptops and Cyberspace access.

CHAPTER ONE

Emergence of the Universe

- Mysterious Dawn
- All from 'No-thing'
- One Source – Singularity
- The Crack of Space-Time
- Light and Darkness
- Earth and Heavens in Six Stages
- Unseen Forces and Realities
- Seven Layers of Earth and Heavens
- Expansion and Diversity
- According to Measures
- The Divine Permeates All
- Relativity of Time
- Air, Water, Fire and Earth
- Signs, Symbols, Metaphors and Similitudes

Mysterious Dawn

There are two sides to the story of creation. One makes sense to our faculty of reason and intellect which science confirms and develops in greater detail. The other story belongs to the mystery of the unknown and the Qur'an addresses this part in some detail. Creation has emerged from non-existence and is suspended in a vast unseen state. The Qur'an states that all of existence occurred in an instant due to the word or command of Allah. The order was 'Be!' and so it was. The speed of creation was such that we can hardly imagine it, for it was much faster than light. Modern astronomers contended that the original blueprints and seeds of creation all occurred within a minute fraction of a second. Human attempts to understand this amazing event bring about some clarification but then lead to greater mysteries. Human reason and rational understanding is only a small part of what there is in creation. What is seen is only a small portion of the vast unseen. Even within the known world and physical rules there are exceptions.

The Qur'an divides human experiences into two zones. One is to do with witnessing experientially and the other is inspiration from the unseen. Islam connects the physical world with the spiritual or metaphysical domain, thus enabling the human being to be complete or wholesome. The believers are described as those who have faith and trust in the unseen and are at peace within their hearts. This total security is far greater than material and earthly security.

The human drive to discover what is not known is relentless and whatever we come to know is only a sample of what is the infinite unknown. The human journey starts from the 'fall' of Adam from the perfect heavenly abode into the earthly zone of all dualities and causal connectedness. It is through the evolvement of consciousness that we journey beyond physical and mental limitations to the source which encompasses all.

God is described as the 'Reality' that knows all other realities in heavens and earth, on land and in the oceans. Not even a leaf falls off a tree unless 'Reality' is aware of it. There is neither a germinating seed in the earth, nor any change in humidity or temperature unless it is according to prescribed patterns. Everything is within the grasp of this supreme 'Reality'.

God's words or commands (power and governance) are countless and ever continuous. Some of these laws and patterns are naturally repetitive and are predictable. Others change with or without discernible reason. The words of God can be imagined as bursts of energies or signals that bring about movement and change within creation.

Divine power or presence is described as enveloping the entire universe and that all of creation emanates from the unseen (metaphysical) and returns back to it. Human beings are encouraged to reflect upon this truth and connect with this Magnificence.

Qur'an References: [30:11] [57:1-3] [3:179] [6:59] [10:20] [11:49] [11:123] [59:22] [27:75] [2:245] [2:268] [13:39] [31:27] [13:12] [36:82]

All from 'No-Thing'

The seamless connectedness between the heavens and earth was split or 'cracked', producing space/time and the earthly state of human consciousness. The original, indistinguishable Oneness lead to apparent outer dispersion, with different entities and creations manifesting. The Prophet was asked what was there before creation and he said 'blindness', implying that it was not discernible or not distinguishable. This also implies that it is a state of 'no-thing' from which everything emerges – a cosmic fog.

The word 'crack' is used in the Qur'an to describe the origin of creation (FTR). Our universe was born from the dark womb of space and time from which countless entities and realities emerged. There may be other parallel universes in existence.

The emergence of space and time is the foundation in creation. Pre-existence, which gave rise to creation and life in its diversity, must have contained the seeds or original patterns which lead to outer manifestations in our universe.

Understanding the origin of life and the human role and direction in creation is at the root of most religions and ideas about God. The human quest regarding the origin of life is amongst the oldest and most potent drives of humanity. Even young children ask how and why they were created and what the meaning of death is.

'No-thingness' is not the same as nothingness. It simply implies lack of material or physical definition or boundaries. It is back to this zone of 'no-thingness' that everything returns at the end of the cycle of creation. A few decades ago science considered particles and fields to be distinct entities. Then came Quantum Theory and its unified view which brought an end to the dualism of matter and energy. This revolutionary idea that there is no material reality brought about a considerable shift in our human understanding of the nature of creation. This mysterious Oneness in the origin of everything that exists and can exist brings about a new perspective to human perception and conduct. As noted earlier, all the 'virtual effects' take place in the so-called 'empty' space between the nucleus of the atom and an orbiting electron. This is the foundation of our so-called real world: a virtual reality that is ever changing and is based on inherent, experiential uncertainty suspended within an 'Absolute Certainty' or truth.

Qur'an References: [79:1-6] [113:1-3] [31:27] [16:77] [5:17] [15:21] [77:3]

1. EMERGENCE OF THE UNIVERSE

One Source – Singularity

The Prophet taught that before creation there was only Allah and nothing else. This implies that in Truth there is none other than the One and whatever we experience is an overflow of grace from that Glorious One. All pluralities are sustained by the ever-present unity.

The Qur'an has numerous descriptions of different levels and states of consciousness in a worldly sense as well as what is described as the hereafter. Human beings as well as other creatures occur in existence as communities and nations on earth as well as in a metaphysical sense in the hereafter. Although each human individual is a separate entity, with a specific fingerprint and a point of birth and death, the essence within each living creature emanates from the universal divine Source. The Qur'an's message is essentially about unity, knowledge and the experience of Oneness in spirit.

Dispersion, separation, individual identity and discernible differences are natural in the physical world and outer experience. Pure consciousness is the source and origin of personal consciousness and the life which all human beings have access to through the soul is a unified field which connects the unseen to the seen and drives us towards inner security and contentment. This is how the cosmic web of Allah holds the universe.

All of the creation follows interlinked patterns which bring about dynamic interactions, cycles of change and connectedness in every aspect of life. These links, connections and interferences are all according to different levels and spheres. There are countless channels of varying degrees of strength and limitations that make 'a whole' out of a multitude of diverse entities and realities. Most old religious texts refer to the package of wholeness as a sacred book. The Qur'an is such a book.

Qur'an References: [67:24] [70:40-41] [114:1-6] [6/1] [10:34] [29:02] [3:09] [6:38] [3/103] [57:22]

The Crack of Space-Time

Absolute Oneness is beyond description, definition or limitation. These are Allah's sacred attributes. Our life and our universe are bracketed by limitations of space and time whose boundaries meet infinities in every direction. Human nature, therefore, is limited by aspects of place and time and yet the most powerful human drive is to go beyond these limitations. Our quest for knowledge, power, beauty and other aspirations like freedom and eternal love all indicate the drive towards the infinite state or zone of experience. We live and function within all limitations but aspire for the limitless. It is as though we strive to get out of the different boxes which include space, time and our mental and emotional constructs. We live with numerous restrictions and limitations whilst in constant quest for the boundless.

Amongst the earliest events in the story of creation is the mysterious occurrence described in the Qur'an where heavens and earth were seamlessly connected and were then torn apart. This tearing, or cracking in the fabric, describes the beginning of the creation of space and time which contains all of existence. The idea of a split or crack is consistently used as metaphor of how something comes out of 'no-thing'. We human beings have self-awareness and therefore an identity which gives us the idea of separation and desire for independence.

All spiritual practices are there to take us back to the original unity through an arc of ascension. The Qur'an tells us that all of creation (heavens and earth) is based upon truth or oneness but veiled by 'otherness'. The goal, therefore, is to perceive unity which is the constant force behind all human endeavours. Rationality and causality is one natural step towards connectedness and unity. We are born within the limitations of space-time, experience the arrow of change and time and then (at death) return back to singularity. Revealed teachings emphasise the need for self-restraint, accountability and the maintenance of boundaries and limitations in the attempts to realise the inner boundlessness. It is as though we need to confirm through our lives (individually and collectively) the limitations of the original 'crack'.

Qur'an References: [42:11] [21:30] [6:1] [7:19] [6:95] [113:1] [7:84] [27:25] [35:1] [39:5] [39:46] [2:229] [78:17]

I. EMERGENCE OF THE UNIVERSE

Light and Darkness

The word for light in Arabic originates from the same root as that of fire (NWR). The Qur'an provides numerous references to different types and qualities of Light. The most common reference is to physically discernible light in nature, such as the light of the moon and the effulgence of the sun. Intelligence and knowledge is another type of light. Then there is the metaphorical light of Allah which brings life to creation and holds the universe – "Allah is the light of the heavens and the earth".

Earthly visible light is a small part of a much wider range of electromagnetic waves and breaks down into rainbow colours which end with ultraviolet at one end and infrared at the other. The Qur'an alludes to numerous levels and spheres of light within the range of human receptivity. Light is often used as a metaphor for what enables us to perceive and experience. We are invited to reflect upon and contemplate natural and mysterious phenomena, which appear to have different facets and qualities. Visible light is composed of photons which have both a particle and a wave function. The Qur'an repeatedly reminds us of the vast unseen worlds and their enormous impact upon what is seen and experientially known. Light and darkness and day and night are also used as metaphors to reflect upon the vast universe which is there to be explored and understood.

Metaphorical light and guidance often accompanies remembrance, awareness, and higher consciousness. A garden or paradise relates to the enjoyable state of contentment and happiness. Fire and hell can be experienced physically in nature but metaphorically relates to forgetfulness, distraction and the lack of enlightenment and realisation of truth. Fire is considered the greatest affliction for it destroys and disintegrates all material substances, whereas light opens up subtler and higher levels of experiences and understanding. Signs and metaphors of the Qur'an are described as the sparks that produce the light of guidance out of the darkness of the 'lower self'.

Qur'an References: [79:29] [51:13] [28:73] [6:96] [7:54] [10:67] [17:12]

Earth and Heavens in Six Stages

Modern astronomers describe for us a most amazing and picturesque vision of how the stars and the galaxies as well as the planets came about. Our solar system was born several billion years after the beginning of creation. It is estimated to be 4.6 billion years ago. The Qur'an does not give us any specific indication as to exactly when creation began or will end. It does however emphasise the relativity of time and that what we count as a thousand years on earth is the equivalent of one day as far as the creator is concerned, or fifty thousand years on earth can be like one day in the hereafter.

The Qur'an describes both the earth as well as other heavenly bodies evolving over a period of six stages, ending with the relatively stable conditions that we experience now. The foundation of our life on earth is considered to be based on water. The six periods or stages in the formation of heavens and earth are also divided into two periods – two and four. The early period of the first two stages are the more fluid and formative stage while stability and ongoingness are established in the subsequent four stages. These four stages of the development of the earth relate to the interdependence of and relationships within the material and sentient life. The word 'smoke' or 'mist' is used to describe the developments of the galactic scene. The final drift of the stars and planets along their course is described as a natural submission of these entities to God's design and wish; whatever begins will return to its origin.

The Qur'an repeatedly emphasises that all human experience is transient, whereas everything in creation flows according to patterns, unfolding one step after another along a cosmic arc of emergence and return to source. In the subtlest of heavens, events can occur at immense speed without clear connection between cause and effect, whereas on earth they play to the tune of space and time and follow cycles of connectedness.

Qur'an References: [78:6-9] [57:4-6] [7:54] [41:9-12] [11:07] [50:38] [52:41] [41:09] [41:12]

1. EMERGENCE OF THE UNIVERSE

Unseen Forces and Realities

Human consciousness lies between the vast galactic dimension and the unseen which envelopes the minute sub-microscopic world of the atom. It is natural for a healthy human being to strive towards knowledge and understanding of the world around us, to grasp the big scale as well as the infinitesimally small.

The heavens are described as being held together by numerous forces acting like pillars or rods whilst most of the stars and galaxies are travelling in prescribed cycles, moving towards their destiny. The vast unseen is described as part of God's governance which from the absolute point of view is ever close and instantaneous. Within the Creator's sanctity (absoluteness) everything is possible instantaneously. "God knows whatever is in the universe and beyond and to Him returns all of creation".

The prophetic voice declares: "I only know what is given to me by the all-Knower and I have no access to the treasuries of what is beyond. I am only given news of the unseen as revealed to me". And, "There is nothing whatsoever in the heavens or the earth unless it is part of a pattern or design already prescribed (in a 'book'). God knows whatever is evident to us and the vast unknown and He is the most wise and subtle. His light permeates the universe."

The human limitation in knowledge and ability is a natural foundation for our drive to strive towards higher consciousness. There is much goodness in discovering heavenly or earthly knowledge. No doubt some of these discoveries are helpful in the pursuit of human ease and comfort but equally they can bring about arrogance, distractions and will be contrary to the purpose of life altogether, which is to submit and draw from the grace of the Life-Giver.

The believers are described as those who are constantly in cautious awareness, secure in the knowledge that what comes to them from the unseen is only appropriate and just. The seeker on the path is confident in God's perfections and mercy and somewhat cautious and apprehensive about one's own thoughts, intentions and actions. The healthy seeker is secure in the belief and trust regarding God's mercy and generosity at all times.

Qur'an References: [16:77] [13:2] [6:59] [6/73] [11:123] [3:179] [6:50] [12:102] [21:49] [36:11] [27:75] [64:18] [2:1-4]

Seven Layers of Earth and Heavens

The earth's seven layers consist of the stratosphere, ionosphere, hemisphere and the biosphere, the earth's crust, mantle and core. The heavenly sky is also described as having seven layers, which could relate to our planetary system, our galaxy, further galaxies, black holes and other bodies. Every layer has its own boundaries whilst connecting with what is above and below it. These layers are also named as channels or pathways of forces, such as gravitational and other less discernible powers. These layers fit with each other and drift along toward their destinies. In traditional Islam names are given to the different realms which are also described as faces of Allah. They are named as hāhūt, lāhūt, jabarūt, malakūt and mulk. The descent is from the most subtle and sublime to the physical earthly.

All the layers that constitute the earth and the heavens are described to be acknowledging and responding to their original design and direction: "they are in full glorification", implying total connectedness without any independent will. There may be multitudes of forces that connect these numerous layers or spheres of creation. God's knowledge and power envelops them all and permeates all that is within them. What appears to us as strange or even beyond imagination has its own forces and drives that govern its behaviour and destiny.

The earth is described as being smooth and made easy for human life. The mountains, valleys, rivers and plains which had occurred later in earth's life correspond with the development of human beings and the rise of human consciousness as it has come to be in the present day. Everything in existence has its own perfect state, connectedness and 'plot'. When Homo Sapiens moved across Asia and what is now Europe a few tens of thousands of years ago, the melting ice and other climatic factors enabled them to cross vast areas of land whilst hugging the coastlines, where food and especially sea protein was abundant and easy to acquire.

Qur'an References: [67:03] [65:12] [41:12] [2/29] [17:44] [41:12] [78:12] [23:17] [67:3] [91:06]

I. EMERGENCE OF THE UNIVERSE

Expansion and Diversity

Astrologers describe the early universe going through an early period of rapid expansion which they label as inflation. At a later period we have millions of stars and galaxies emerging with their identities. The Qur'an describes the creation and construction of heavens as "ever-expanding and widening". It also mentions the mysterious occurrence and life of stars and highlights their position (for we know they are moving at an immense speed) and considers this state of affairs as a most enormous and awesome event to be reflected upon.

Diversity on earth is found in every created form. Colours, forms and textures come in countless varieties. The colour of human skin varies vastly yet in essence all human beings follow a similar blueprint. Creatures and animals equally come in endless varieties, shapes and colours. Herbage, plants and trees not only differ in their life cycles, but their habitat and produce that benefits other creatures are also multifarious. Several plants, insects and animals are mentioned in the Qur'an as samples of creational diversity on earth. As plants grow to their fruition they announce their state by the evident change in colour, form and shape, and then they wither, yellow, decay and return to their constituent elements, their original material origin. The earth's crust, rocks and mountains are described as having every possible colour and ray, from jet black to crystal white.

Some fascinating detail is given about a few creatures such as ants, spiders, birds and cattle. The Qur'an highlights the amazing process within the honey bee that produces a nourishing liquid with different colours and benefits to human beings as well as other creatures. All these creations and existences are permeated by the power of God, some of which are seen and discernible by us and much of it not. The universe is held together by powers that are far more subtle than forces discernible or measureable by us. Generally 'angelic' power is described as the cause of many of the subtle and unknown forces that govern the universe.

Qur'an References: [30:22] [16:69] [35:28] [39:21] [35:27] [6:141] [2:255] [4:97] [51:47] [77:3] [56:75]

According to Measures

God has created whatever is known and unknown according to appropriate and relevant measures and boundaries. The sun, moon and other stars drift in a prescribed orbit according to cycles and phases. Nothing whatsoever exists in the universe unless it follows a certain direction which can change in time, according to interactions with other forces and realities. Mankind, who is defined as God's steward on earth, is held responsible to ensure respect of nature and interconnected sensitivities in earthly matters. He is ordered to tread gently upon the earth and regard himself as being in transition through his time here, returning eventually to the celestial realm.

Day and night follow according to the earth's rotation around its tilted axis, thus producing the change of seasons. All earthly and heavenly change can be traced to interacting forces and therefore to reasons and causes that we often can understand. Likewise it is always easier to reflect upon a past event and make sense of what happened after the event. We also constantly strive to read the future in order to be prepared for new situations that may arise. Human beings are deeply programmed to love and desire eternity and to strive for physical immortality. We know that all bodies and matter will be recycled whereas the light which causes life carries on. We are both mortal (physically) and immortal (spiritually).

The Qur'an and the Prophetic message remind us that we as human beings naturally like to measure and count and that after death we will be held responsible to account for our earthly life and all our intentions and actions. The event of resurrection is a proof of the perfect justice of the Creator. Those who have lived on earth striving towards God-consciousness and constant awareness will experience the garden where the provisions therein are beyond measure. Our life on earth constantly follows the balance between different entities, limitations and interactions, whereas the life of the soul, after departure from its body, is not subject to these laws; it is another zone of life. The soul is sacred in nature but carries traces of its life on earth when it was a prisoner in the human body and mind.

Qur'an References: [06:59] [15:21] [78:29] [73/26] [90:05] [65:03] [25:02] [36:39] [10:05] [13:21] [38:53] [78:36] [40:40]

1. EMERGENCE OF THE UNIVERSE

The Divine Permeates All

Our life on earth has a measureable aspect. Much of what concerns us is visible, discernible and measurable – subject to space and time. We follow patterns and cycles of emanation and return within the constant pool of energy that does not increase or reduce. It follows clearly the two laws of thermodynamics: the law of conservation of energy and entropy. Then there is another aspect of life which is sometimes considered as supernatural but which within its own zone flows according to perfect divine laws. At the point when these two zones of our life meet great scientific discoveries and spiritual insights can bring about fascinating ideas and theories regarding the nature of life and existence.

The whole universe is enveloped by the power, knowledge and will of Allah. God is before everything, after the end of everything and is the power behind all manifestations and all that is unseen. The universe can thus be considered as an extension and manifestation of the sacred Reality. It is a grace that can enable human beings to come to know that almost unknowable truth – Allah. Every aspect of creation within the universe follows its destiny and all of these destinies link in subtle ways to their origin and ultimate destiny, which meet in the original Oneness. The earth's destiny is to settle down from its original gaseous, fluid and material states and stabilise for life to emerge. Human destiny is to attain, by direct experience, the Light of lights which is the ultimate source and essence of the whole universal story.

Every entity follows the arrow of time by having a beginning and an end. Human intentions, actions and earthly endeavours are considered as secondary to what is potentially possible and allowed to happen. What actions we undertake can only follow a possibility that was potentially already there. The outcome of good or bad is relative and sometimes they reverse in position according to our perspective. What is good on one occasion can be bad in another. Increase in worldly attachment and concern is likely to bring about a decrease in spiritual or higher consciousness and God-awareness. Whatever plans and projects we have are secondary to the original Divine Will which will always prevail. For that reason religious people often reflect upon God's Will in the hope that they make their will subservient to it. After all, we always desire success. Wrong intentions and actions will generate their symmetrical effect of suffering upon the perpetrator and those who are within that domain of influence. All human plans and hopes will fade to nothing unless they unfold along the path of God-consciousness and enlightenment.

Allah's wills and plans are mostly unknown to us except for that which is immediate and close by. Through diverse angelic powers the different levels of realities and outcomes appear to us. Ultimately, therefore, God's intentions will prevail at all times even though we struggle hard in our own way and often mistakenly believe that we are acting independently. The power of the magnificent Lord is before, after, and within all that goes on in creation on earth and in heavens. In truth there is only the Lord, Allah!

Qur'an References: [17:60] [65:12] [3:120] [4:126] [3:54] [13:24] [27:50] [14:46] [3:54] [10:21] [7:99] [35:10] [35:43] [57:03]

Relativity of Time

Human consciousness is such that all of our experiences are relative with regards to time and place. For a child a month is fairly long; a mother can measure the growth in her child almost on a daily basis. For a sixty year old person even a year seems to pass by speedily. In our day-to-day experiences we sometimes feel that time has passed rapidly and yet some other times it is very slow going, even boring.

The human cycle of birth and death is framed within space-time and the ultimate, constant drive is to experience a permanent state that is not constrained by space and time. Immortality is a reflection of this natural innate human desire. Adam in the garden was tempted by the suggestion of Satan (the voice of personal consciousness) seeking immortality. Thus the descent to earth and the zone of space-time, death and suffering become unacceptable. The love of eternity and infinite perfection radiates within us from the immortal soul in the heart – God's residing agent!

There are several examples given to us in the Qur'an both in this life and after death indicating the relativity of time. When the people in the cave were asked how long they had been in there (probably 309 years), they thought it may have been merely one day. The same thing happened to another traveller who had died for a hundred years and when he came to consciousness he thought it had been a day or a part of the day. The proof of the length of his absence was the decayed food with him and his dead donkey. Our earthly measures of time and the cycles of seasons are helpful to regulate our life in our earthly nursery. Our earthly and human consciousness requires references to time and place, whereas our divine reality or soul is free of all such limitations.

The day of reckoning or resurrection is highlighted in the Qur'an and is described as being very close to us at all times. The human tendency, however, is to give more attention to the physical and material world. The day of reckoning is described as a state wherein an individual cannot be helped by anyone and is stripped of any ability to act or exercise will. In that state, the whole of creation will be directly aware of the eternal truth or the presence of the Lord of the universe. For the souls that have been distracted on earth, that day is described as being of great confusion and fear. Those who were not aware of the day of reckoning on earth will be in utter bewilderment and sorrow. In that state, every self (ego and soul) will experience the cumulative life of their intentions and actions on earth.

Our earthly zone of life follows a relatively regulated flow of times and cycles. Life after the end of this phase is described as "that of a day, in it is the equivalent of a thousand years as we count". Also, resurrection is given the metaphor where one day is the equivalent of 50,000 years (on earth).

The seeker of truth is reminded to always visualise the end of what is normally considered to be real any minute! This is how awareness of the moment connects with timeless consciousness. The relative and the absolute are ever connected.

Qur'an References: [70:4-7] [22:47] [23:113] [2:259] [82:18-19] [83:06] [2:259] [22:47] [45:34] [3:30] [16:77] [54:0-2]

I. EMERGENCE OF THE UNIVERSE

Air, Water, Fire and Earth

For centuries the elements of air, water, earth and fire were regarded as the principle substances from which all that is on earth is made. During the past century numerous elements have been discerned and their basic atomic constituency and tendencies became known. Stable elements which have their own specific atomic weight and number are in excess of 92+ entities. The smallest chemical element is that of the hydrogen atom with a simple nucleus and one electron orbiting it. The larger and more complex atoms follow to very large and unstable states.

Fire and air are connected quite clearly, where matter or water is in a gaseous state. Water (vapour) becomes diffused with air and is experienced simply as moist air. Water solidifies when it freezes and curiously increases in volume, whereas all other materials when cooled shrink. All material entities can also exist in a gas state albeit not always in a stable condition. All of these four substances inter-relate with each other and coexist as well as nullify or modify each other (such as water and fire, earth and air, water and air, earth and water).

Fire in the Qur'an is a metaphor for a state of maximum disturbance and destruction. Whatever is burning is being reduced to its original elements. Jinn are the other earthly creation whose nature is that of fire and smoke, whereas humans are predominantly earth and water. When earth and water is graced by a mysterious sacred light which we call a soul or spirit, the human entity emerges into its being. Water is the natural substance that brings about visible life on earth at numerous levels of sentiency.

Air, wind or breeze has life-giving properties such as carrying down rain, as well as destructive power, as when it brings hurricanes and tornados. The Qur'an describes several historical events in Arabia where strong and famous nations were destroyed by severe winds, earthquakes or other natural disasters. The Arabic word for air is the same as that of the egotistic whims and confusing desires (HWA). The endeavours of those who follow the whims of their ego are described as ash being blown by the wind.

Life on earth has been described as another metaphor: the rains that have come down from the heavens bring the earth to life and produce countless varieties of herbage and creatures – for a while whatever comes to existence will also cease to be. Only the divine light of the Creator is ever constant and everything else in the universe is an overflow from that essence and returns to it. The awakened human being recognizes all the changing entities and creations whilst in constant reference to the mysterious reality that is not subject to any change. Whoever is conscious of the sacred presence and curbs the lower self from its distractions and illusions is at the edge of the boundless state of bliss, happiness or paradise.

Qur'an References: [36:80] [67:30] [79:40] [14/43] 32:09] [14:18] [69:06] [02:164] [25:48] [56:89] [02:217] [02:257] [03:10] [04:145] [15:27] [24:35-37] [30:20] [22:05] [10:24] [21:30]

Signs, Symbols, Metaphors and Similitudes

The Qur'an is described as the book of signs, symbols, metaphors and similitudes. Reflecting upon the diversity of creations, the universe, the differences between day and night and all other natural events that regulate life is a great opening for those who seek to understand. These signs and symbols are like maps or prescriptions which can only be useful if they are read, considered, and followed with faith and humbleness at heart. Good intentions, clarity in mind and purity at heart are necessary conditions. Trust and belief in the unseen, as well as in life after death, are necessary to remove the dark egotistic veils. A healthy intellect, rationality and the ability to intelligently reflect upon interlinking ideas and thoughts are essential. Hearing and sight are both outer senses as well as inner faculties which lead to intuition and spiritual insight. Sacred signs and maps become evident for those who are ready to read them. God's signs have been potentized by the light of truth within the heart of the seeker who will benefit from the full meaning of visible and unseen creations.

The metaphor of Adam in the garden and the rise of his desire for eternity, and therefore his descent to earthly consciousness, is followed by numerous metaphors regarding human conduct on earth. A person who is employed by different, opposing employers is very different from one who works for one clear and just employer. Whoever is entangled with conflicting worldly attachments, desires and needs is not the same as he who follows the light of guidance from his pure heart or soul. Those who do not believe and recognise the supremacy of God are like those whose actions are like ashes in strong winds – they will have no effect. Those who do not refer to and rely upon God's power and will are like the spider taking refuge in its flimsy web. Our natural tendency to want secure homes on earth is only an aspect of our desire to feel secure within our own heart, irrespective of outer circumstances. The righteous people who spend their time and their wealth in the way of truth and justice are like a seed that grows to yield seven corn ears. Within each one of them is a hundred seeds. Good deeds always multiply and wrong ones will only generate their equivalent. Earthly and heavenly signs become clear guidelines for the thoughtful, reflective beings, especially when they are in gratitude and their hearts are content and at peace. The more we read and follow the sacred signs around us through messages that reach us via our senses, minds and hearts, the sharper our intellect and spiritual insight will become. The purpose of this life is to be awakened to the source of life from which everything has manifested, by which all is sustained, and to which everything returns.

The Qur'an emphasises that we should reflect upon signs on the horizons as well as within our own selves. Deep reflection will lead to the abandonment of all desires and will enable us to realise the mysterious unity that permeates all that movement and change within the universe. The conclusion to all human quests is the experience of the One.

Qur'an References: [69:38-39] [3:190] [30:25] [2:17] [2:26] [14:18] [18:54] [29:41] [16:75-76] [30:28] [39:29] [29:43] [16:16] [2:248] [16:11] [16:13] [16:65] [16:67] [15:77] [29:35] [2:252] [7:58] [24:61]

CHAPTER TWO

Life on Earth and its Diversity

- Basic Substances
- Cosmic Forces
- Waters of Life
- Life on Dead Earth
- Day and Night
- Light of Consciousness
- Dualities, Pairs and Polarities
- Oppositions and Complementarities
- Plants, Grains, Trees and Fruit
- Insects, Birds, Animals, Individuals and Groups
- Angels as Messengers
- Jinn, Satans and Humans
- Everything Towards a Destiny
- Cycles and Orbits
- Planets and Stars

Basic Substances

In most ancient cultures and especially the East, the basic elements of creation were considered to be air, fire, water and earth. Nowadays we know that there are over a hundred basic elements, 92 of which are natural and exist normally on earth, whereas the others do exist but are not stable. We also know that atoms can connect with each other creating molecules and that living cells are composed of these somewhat larger entities. Sub-atomic particles are numerous and some of these energy bursts can only be explained by mathematical theories and the mysterious world of quantum physics. From a human point of view we can understand that we have both a material structure as well as a subtle energy provider which regulates life. In other words, we have a material reality as well as an unseen soul or source of consciousness, like light which is a combination of a photon (a particle) and a wave.

Water constitutes the greatest percentage of both the human make-up as well as what is on the surface of the earth. The earth's stability is balanced by the relationships between gas (air), fire (heat), water, all the mineral substances and energy fields and forces seen and unseen.

The Qur'an describes creation as partly discernible and partly unseen. It warns that much of existence is beyond our mental capacity to comprehend or understand; only to Allah belong the inner secrets and deep origins. The outer worlds are samples of the mysterious inner realities, and they only become clearer to us after death and the loss of our outer senses.

The Qur'an too declares that there is not even an atom on earth or in the heavens, or even smaller than that or larger, that is not governed by the Lord of creation. The patterns and laws of this governance are described as the 'sacred book'. Whatever is known and unknown belong to God, who permeates all from beginning to end. Human beings are created from base materials and substances but are graced with a drive to experience goodness materially, mentally and spiritually.

Qur'an References: [6:43] [4:76] [2:268] [7:22] [24:21] [67:5]

Cosmic Forces

Materially all creation on earth is made from star dust which had fallen from galactic debris over billions of years to form the solar system. Equally all forms of life relate and connect with all powers and forces in the cosmos. The story is often blurred and unclear at the boundaries and outer limits. But close at hand in space and time we can understand most natural events, causalities, relationships and correlations. Stability and security are attainable in relative terms and are close by. The further we look in space and time the more obscure the situation becomes.

Life on earth is due to the interaction of light, water and other forces which may be replicated in other parts of the universe or multiverses in different ways. The same substances and physical forces that regulate our planetary system may operate elsewhere with some variations unfamiliar to us. We may feel we are unique but that is due to a presence of the mysterious soul within our hearts which gives us the illusion of being extra special. We are terrestrial creatures of celestial origin.

Throughout our history many people have considered themselves to be superior to others or God-chosen. The light of the soul, which has within it all the attributes and qualities of God, gives this illusion of being extra special on a personal or collective basis. There is some truth in that exclusivity, but we need to consider that all other human beings carry the same life-giving entity. Divine attributes engulf the universe and bring about qualities that interconnect and relate with each other. Each of these attributes has special characteristics but the essence is the original Divine Light itself. Like the rainbow, each colour has its own frequency but all colours are part of the same electromagnetic field.

The entire universe and its components are held by intricate forces and balances which include human consciousness and self-reflection. The ultimate state of goodness in human conduct is not to disturb the balance of nature but to work alongside it and, wherever possible, to enhance it. All power and strength, knowledge and ability emanate from the original sacred source. Angels and many other non-discernible entities or metaphysical realities are part of the cosmic forces that regulate whatever there is within the cosmos. Infinite varieties of messages and signals criss-cross the universe and only a small portion of these are known or measurable.

Qur'an References: [41:39][14:32][35:9][51:1-4][52:1-6][55:1-13][22:65][11:66][51:58][16:2][22:75]

Waters of Life

A few billion years ago the doors of the heavens had opened up and poured an incessant amount of water upon the earth. Thus the ever-recycled water on earth is constant in quantity. The Qur'an encourages reflection upon how this water came down from the heavens upon a dead earth and gave rise to life and all the herbage and creatures. Water is at the core of all of life on earth. "His throne was upon water" implies that life on earth is part of the sacred domain where divine governance penetrates every aspect. The water that poured down is described as having flowed into whatever depressions there were. Subsequently the earth began to vibrate due to the interaction of water and light from which life emerged and ultimately the earth became green. The Qur'an describes how this heavenly water gave earth its new life and is the cause of all the diverse fruits and grains and other provisions.

Water, wind, light, earth and fire are all linked in the Qur'an, which declares that when lightning occurs, people's emotions will be mixed between fear (of being struck by lightning) and hope (that rain will enhance life).

Physical water will clearly produce physical growth of creation on earth, but this is also a reference to what could be considered as metaphorical water that brings about purity (in mind and heart) and therefore awakening to God-consciousness. This special favour is labelled as 'heavenly pure water', as well as 'water of grace'. Since water is the source of material life on earth it also contains within it powers that are subtle or metaphysical. From ancient times ritual ablution had been practised by older cultures. Baptism is a key practice for Christians while in Islam ritual ablution is a necessary preliminary act for prayer. By our awareness of the significance of water we consciously acknowledge the original source of life – seen and unseen.

Qur'an References: [25:48] [2:164] [50:9] [24:45] [30:24] [22:63] [32:27] [54:11] [2:22] [8:11] [10:24] [11:7] [13:17] [21:30] [41:39]

2. LIFE ON EARTH AND ITS DIVERSITY

Life on Dead Earth

After a few billion years, from its birth the earth began to stabilise and settle down. With the suitable temperature, pressure, humidity, light and other factors, a few hundred million years ago, cellular life began. Due to the earth's wobble, the changes of day and night, the numerous global currents in the upper atmosphere as well as in the oceans, different environments and micro-climates helped to bring about the creation of great varieties of microscopic living organisms. The numerous and natural earthly upheavals and atmospheric changes also enhanced the diversity of creation. Cosmologists estimate the birth of our solar system at 4600 million years ago. On a time scale taking 13 years ago as the beginning of the universe, human beings as we know them today would have come about two days ago!

The Qur'an reminds us that in the same way that the earth was the cradle of life, so too will there be another phase which will again bring back the experience of life after death. The signs of how this dead earth came to life, producing countless varieties of herbage and animals is a good case to reflect upon when we consider what may come later. The same way as the living came out of the dead so will a new life emerge from the dead. The earth is simply our little perch from which these intricately interlinked events take place.

All living entities have two stages to their lives: one is physical and the other is spiritual. The physical is based upon water and conversion of energy. The spiritual part is based upon what is conventionally referred to as spirits or souls. Plant spirits are far more adaptable and flexible than complex animals. Most plants do not die by cutting a limb or two, whereas as mammals we have a central organising faculty which breaks down the entire system if damaged. All of what goes on around us is helpful to expand our imaginative faculty, intellect and consciousness. All living and dead entities on earth can be regarded as ladders, climbing up towards higher consciousness and the realisation of the Absolute.

Qur'an References: [43:11] [50:11] [79:31] [24:45] [50:6-7] [36:33] [6:95] [77:26] [43:11]

Day and Night

The most prevalent earthly cyclical duality is day and night, which are both experientially real as well as metaphorical. Most of us experience clear and obvious situations (day) as well as dark and obscure uncertainties (night). Day and night represent action and interaction with creation as well as withdrawal and periods of rest, respite and body-mind rebalancing and renewal.

Although day and night are in a constant cycle replacing each other, their duration and qualities, such as temperature and pressure, change and vary according to different parts of the world and different seasons. The Arctic day is several months, as is its night. The life of those living within it or close to it is adjusted to that unusual rhythm. Near the Equator the yearly difference between day and night is barely noticeable for there is hardly any change in the seasons. Day and night represent the two halves of what we call one whole day. They are two clearly different experiences within one day – a metaphor of dualities emanating from Oneness, one day with two sides to it!

Like the earth's spherical shape, day and night follow and replace each other as though in a circular chase. The night is usually calm whereas the day is full of activity. The day is a realm of earthly connection with all the senses, while night belongs to peace and stillness and is a refuge from worldly interactions. Prayers and meditation are therefore easier at night. The mysterious night journey of the Prophet which took place in a flash of an eye from Makkah to Jerusalem occurred in the unseen or during darkness. The light of the Qur'an and its meaning and message descended also upon the Prophet during the 'Night of Power' or 'Determination'. That event was immense and weighty. It is not easy to understand that the entire universe is held together by a unique Oneness.

All of life's experiences are metaphors and preparations for what comes after death. Sleeping at night is considered as a mini death. We long for good, deep sleep and yet we are fearful of death. This paradox could be an incentive to practice mindlessness or oblivion through meditation, which takes us to the edge of death. To avoid the issue is a denial of the most natural event and becomes the source of much fear and superstition. To die to the outer world is to be at the edge of eternal life.

Qur'an References: [2:164] [6:60] [10:67] [11:114] [13:3] [7:12] [22:61] [25:47] [39:05] [52:49] [44:3] [97:1-5]

Light of Consciousness

Being alive or conscious is described in the Qur'an as being at two levels with regards to human beings. One is physical and biological life or consciousness, and the other level is to do with God-consciousness or enlightenment. People who are living only at the biological level are described as those who are in darkness, or who are veiled from truth, or who are simply following their egotistic plans and directions which will ultimately lead them to misery and sorrow. They plan and plot and do not have the reflectiveness and referencing as to where that would lead them. They only deceive themselves but they do not have self-awareness of that deception. They think they are on a clear path, whereas in fact they are at a loss and they do not perceive it.

Those who follow their faith and act appropriately have the basic qualification to emerge from the levels of darkness of the self into the light of the heart. It is this friendliness with truth and their faith and trust in God that will eventually enable them to emerge into awakened life or enlightenment. It is God who guides to this ultimate light whoever is ready for and capable of it. It is He and the angels which are the agents who enable human beings to come out of the darkness of the earth (body and mind) into the heavenly lights (heart and soul). As for those who do not have that desire, readiness or capacity to be illumined, they will remain adrift and confused.

The Prophet's role is described as a witnesser of truth, the giver of good news and the warner, the guide to enlightenment and a constant beacon of light, even if no one heeds the message. The Prophet's desire is to help all of creation attain God-consciousness and to lead humanity from its base nature of darkness to light.

Mature human beings who are without living faith and a path in life are described as dead metaphorically without them feeling it. Then there are the challenging statements from the Qur'an: "Is it the same who was dead and was given life and a light to navigate, is he the same as others?" "Is the blind man the same as he who can see well?" "Is darkness and light the same?" The purpose and drive in humanity is to come to know the ever-present sacred light within the heart. That is the source of constant joy and the ultimate source of guidance.

Qur'an References: [30:02] [11:82] [2:74] [24:3] [99:7-8] [67:17] [2:22] [34:2] [10:101] [11:123] [3:179] [14:2] [19:90] [63:7] [57:2] [10:5] [16:21] [13:16] [27:50] [6:123] [3:69] [2:257] [5:15] [14:5] [24:35] [33:43] [65:11] [24:40] [16:8] [33:46] [6:122]

Dualities, Pairs and Polarities

Whatever we experience on earth has two aspects to it. Within creation there is balance and symmetry between opposites, seen and unseen. Matter is balanced by anti-matter, day meets night, and death is a natural end of birth. Whatever is considered good has within it the seed of 'bad'. The Qur'an sums up all of this by saying "Glory be to the Creator of all pairs from what had emerged from the earth and your own selves and from what you do not know." The earthly realm, mulk, and that which precedes it, malakūt, are subject to differentiations and dualities, whereas the subtler higher realms – Jabarūt and Lāhūt – are more unified forces and have not yet bifurcated.

We are warned to exercise cautious awareness and seek God-consciousness throughout our lives in order to be liberated from innate insecurities and fears. All human beings have been created in pairs from the same blueprint. This complementarity between male and female is like a natural metaphor of emanation from One Source into duality and multiplicity, striving for unity. The Qur'an describes that most of creation on earth are in pairs.

From a religious point of view, we are reminded that there cannot be two Gods or masters regulating and permeating this most complex universe. When we reflect upon the creation of dualities and pluralities and the futility of constantly striving to satisfy desires, we may conclude that the ultimate purpose of life is to realise the ever-present Oneness which leads us to Itself. The metaphor of Adam in the garden and his desire to attain immortality led to the descent to the earth of change and cyclical return. Adam's offspring need to struggle against the ego and the idea of being independent or separate from the One Source. It is desired that this abode belongs to opposites and that the awakened human being will transcend that state, such that he may come to regard, as the Qur'an indicates, his enemy as a dear friend.

Dualities repeat in every aspect of life, including birth and death. We are born physically and with spiritual enlightenment we are metaphorically born again. The same applies to death. There is the physical death on earth and there is a second death which includes all of creation leading to the resurrection in the hereafter. The death of the universe ends all of existence as it returns to its mysterious Oneness.

Qur'an References: [2:35] [36:36] [55:17] [4:1] [55:52] [51:49] [81:7] [26:7] [16:51] [40:11] [2:164] [31:10] [45:4] [2:36] [7:24] [41:34]

Oppositions and Complementarities

Human life revolves around relative relationships and values energised by a mysterious origin. The Qur'an reminds us that from amongst our closest family there can emerge enmity, but that if we can forgive and overcome shortcomings we are closer to understanding Oneness. Wealth, power and offspring will challenge us – they are the tests and trials on earth. All challenges of dualities dissolve when the lens of inner unity becomes our main viewpoint. Then we realise that opposites as well as complementary issues have emerged from the same origin and that they will return to that source.

Enmity, conflict and wars are all due to mistaken personal as well as collective identity. All 'otherness' has emerged from Oneness and is sustained by it. Separation and duality are earthly covers over the ever-present powers and unity. The Qur'an declares that human beings were initially one people but then with spreading out in the earth, differences began to occur when cultures, language and ideas and specific values emerged as part of life. With human evolvement outer differences seem considerable, but if we look deeply into human drives and desires we find a commonality in the quest for sustainable goodness and wholesomeness in life. Ultimately sameness in essence is thinly covered by outer differences and biographies.

Enlightenment means having constant access to the inner joy of the soul, which the Qur'an describes as the heavenly garden experienced here and now. Similarities and differences are described as existing at every level of creation: minerals, stones, mountains, plants, trees as well as fruits and all living creatures. We see similarities, differences and complementarities throughout existence. The insects that pollinate the flowers have co-evolved over millions of years and are an example of complementarity. In the earth's atmosphere opposite forces meet and bring about a new emergence, such as within clouds, winds, lightning, and other phenomena. Often we see how the opposites end up complementing and reinforcing each other. At times similarities end up showing differences. Life is balanced in the dynamic of what appears as opposites.

Qur'an References: [64:14-15] [6:99] [59:14] [2:253] [10:19] [11:118] [49:13] [47:6] [08:63] [24:43] [37:173]

Plants, Grains, Trees and Fruit

More than twenty ayat of the Qur'an refer to numerous plants, fruits, grains and herbage that form a part of life on earth. Palm trees, dates, olives, pomegranates, grapes and figs are specifically mentioned, while fruits in general are also referred to in different contexts on several occasions. Barley, wheat, rice, millet, lentils, gourds, onions, mustard, tamarind, garlic and other types of seasonal beans were known and used in Arabia at the time of the Prophet. The Qur'an refers to these grains and seeds in a broad sense as part of agriculture. Specific reference is made regarding plants appearing in pairs, and as sharing similarity in roots and origin, as well as dissimilarities. The Arab traders had considerable access to products that came from the Far East via the Silk Route or from the south (Ethiopia and Yemen). Surrounded by the desert the Arabs were very partial to green pastures, oases and gardens. The trade route up to Damascus was naturally favoured by the merchants partly because of the luxuriant fields and orchards around that ancient city.

Apart from utility value and human consumption, plants are also used as a metaphor for how good things can multiply on earth with care and goodwill. To be in gratitude and reflectiveness is also associated with bounties on earth. This also comes with the warning not to waste or transgress. We are challenged to think about multitudes of plants and greens all emerging from the same soil and the same water. The Qur'an refers to the one water, which may also imply a life force that physical water facilitates. Truffles and other self-seeding fungi were considered as earthly samples of 'heavenly' gifts and bounty.

In addition to everyday feed, plants were also used for medicinal purposes, health restriction and healing. The early health practitioners in Islam combined local knowledge with what came from the Mediterranean, as well as India and farther afield. Muslim doctors accepted and absorbed useful practices from far and wide; Greek and Ayurvedic practices were integrated and absorbed in the culture.

Qur'an References: [55:11] [55:52] [55:68] [80:28] [16:11] [2:61] [43:73] [95:1] [2:57] [5:146] [5:16] [5:47] [13:4] [17:90] [2:266] [36:34]

Insects, Birds, Animals, Individuals and Groups

The Qur'an cites the example of a gnat or a mosquito representing a small but complete entity following its programme with ease and efficiency. Smaller bacteria and viruses propagate, mutate and multiply with ease. Every form of life is seeking growth, expansion and continuity on earth. Complex insects adapt to their environment for protection as well as ease of securing provision. The spider with its exceptionally flimsy dwelling is a parable for human attempts to establish secure homes and cities on earth. We are reminded to visit ancient sites of bygone peoples and their attempts to build secure dwellings and monuments with pride and defiance. Human beings relentlessly seek power and status and thus are driven to construct buildings and social structures that appear durable and impressive. The architecture of our houses of parliament or banks are good examples of this inevitable human ambition to uphold the myth of security.

Everything that exists follows paths to their destiny. Many of the species and entities have a social life and are connected by bonds of community. They all follow patterns and directions with a measured stability and strength as well as adaptability. The altruism or self-sacrifice of ants is part of the preference for the survival of the species over the individual. Human genes may exhibit a trait of intense love for survival (which have been described as 'selfish' genes) but the evolved self which has awakened to the truth of the eternal soul will have no fear regarding death.

Certain evolved beings like the Prophet Solomon could understand the soundless communication of insects and other creatures. When his army was about to destroy some ants' dwellings, he understood how the ants rushed away to protect their nests from being trampled on. The Prophet David was also given the intuitive understanding of how birds exist in a state of glorification and how to utilise the strength of metals, rocks and mountains.

In the story of human evolvement, cattle has played a big role for many thousands of years, leading human beings to become cattle herders and then settlers, relying on agriculture and later on industry and technology. Most creatures have special skills that enable them to achieve their purpose in life. Human beings need both outer and inner skills to be content.

Qur'an References: [6:38] [42:29] [16:79] [21:79] [24:41] [27:16] [105:03] [6:38] [27:18] [29:41] [2:26] [16:5] [16:66]

Angels as Messengers

From pre-historic times human beings have had a great attraction to the unknown and invisible entities such as Angels. For thousands of years they have been represented as messengers, guardians and heavenly help and guidance. Christians, Jews and Muslims retell the stories of the Angels that came to the Prophet Ibrahim, the difference being that in the Hebrew account they partook of his offerings and hospitality. According to Islamic tradition Angels do not eat as we do. Also, Satan in Islam is considered to be a Jinn in origin. The Jewish idea about Angels was developed in Babylon, where Zoroastrianism was the main religion and Angels formed a part of the belief. Although it is recognised that Angels are neither male nor female we find in most of the representations, especially in Christianity, they appear as male.

The Qur'an describes Angels as being at different levels of proximity or distance to God, as well as possessing a range of powers, strength and abilities. Angels are described as agents and messengers with wings of different numbers and strength. The Qur'an reinforces the belief in Angels and other heavenly forces both in this world and the hereafter. These are all Allah's creation and His ways that will lead to greater knowledge of Him and his presence. With belief in God we are told that Angels will give us aid and strength. It is God Himself who transmits all the graces and blessings upon creation and Angels help to bring upon us light in the earthly darkness. This is where material entities become illumined and sentient.

The Qur'an refers to other forces besides the Angels as messengers who follow sets of patterns and pathways already prescribed. They are referred to as 'heavenly' forces and their knowledge or understanding is beyond us. These heavenly soldiers operate within the entire universe as well as upon earth. God's messengers who are not constrained by the limitations of space and time record all of our intentions and actions during our lifetime.

Angels became visible to many of the Prophets for it was mostly through them that revelation took place. These messengers appeared to the ancient prophets such as Ibrahim, Lot and others, giving them news and directions. Angels and heavenly messengers occasionally appeared disguised as human beings or other creatures.

Qur'an References: [6:93] [3:125] [22:75] [41:30] [4:136] [33:43] [35:01] [48:4] [74:31] [10:21] [29:33] [5:32]

2. LIFE ON EARTH AND ITS DIVERSITY

Jinn, Satans and Humans

There are several intangible creations that occasionally and mysteriously connect with us. These are mostly energic entities that have their own life story, direction and boundaries. Human consciousness is potentially able to conceive much of what is on earth and can have some ideas about what lies beyond. We evolve from physical sensations to subtler mental, intellectual and spiritual domains.

Angels have different levels of power and complexity; their nature is that of light. Archangels have impacted upon prophets to produce revelations and miraculous deeds. Angels connect with humans at levels beyond the mind and senses – closer to the sixth sense or a hazy dream. They do not have a free will or the higher levels of consciousness that we can access.

Jinn (spirits) are similar creatures to human beings except that their main substance is fire instead of earth. They are unseen and in locations away from human beings, although their proximity can be felt on special occasions. Their basic nature is that of fire and smoke. When they heard the Qur'an some of them submitted to its truth and others (like humans) rejected it. The social life and hierarchy of Jinn is not dissimilar to that of human beings. The Prophet Solomon had power over them and used them to establish his kingdom on earth. Conventional wisdom holds that one not be concerned or involved with these and other 'magical' and unseen creations. People who dabble with Jinni powers run the risk of entrapment and possession. It is best to avoid this charm of 'power' temptation.

Satan, Iblis, the devil and other demonic entities relate to the dark side of human life and its negative aspects that impede spiritual progress. It was satanic energy that disturbed Adam's perfect state of bliss in the Garden by mental arousal and inquisitiveness about the tree or meaning of eternity, or the state of eternity. Adam was already in a state wherein there was no consciousness of 'otherness'; and in this he reflected the quality of soul consciousness, rather than conditioned consciousness. The human soul is in perfect contentment and joy until it is coupled with the body or mind and entered into the cycle of birth or death.

Qur'an References: [72:1-2] [35:1] [20:117] [55:14-16] [50:17-18]

Everything Towards a Destiny

Whatever begins in creation will also end. The whole universe is governed by countless interacting patterns and governing laws and principles. These are God's decrees. Destinies are what we experience at different stages of our lives, ending with a final destiny when the body separates from the soul – death. We can change aspects of our destinies with attention and appropriate action, for we have been given the discriminating faculties of what is appropriate for us and what is not, in the short term as well as long term. Numerous verses in the Qur'an describe these challenges to us so as to refer back or return to the original purpose of life – the knowledge of God. Destinies can change as we strive towards God's will, but there are also specific creational principles that are constant and are referred to as the original sacred 'tablets'.

We are all challenged to attain a certain level of clarity so that we connect the seen with the unseen and ultimately return to the sacred precinct which is ever present. Individuals, as well as groups of human beings, can thus exercise will and reach a better outcome in life. Successful transaction is to move from the lower tendencies of the ego to the higher lights of the soul. We emerged due to God's grace and to the same essence we shall all return. Our life is a preparation for a goodly return. That destiny is desired by all but the path needs to be discerned and followed.

Human beings are propelled towards a better quality life: ease comfort, peace, friendliness, security, etc. Thus we all have a desire to anticipate the future and to be prepared for what is coming. From the earliest prehistorical times, we looked for signs from the heavens as well as on earth in order to be prepared as well as to have hope. The development of astrology as well as reading signs by more sensitive or qualified human beings has been a very popular endeavour.

Qur'an References: [7:174] [7:168] [13:39] [4:97] [78:40] [35:29] [89:28] [2:28] [28:88] [41:21] [65:3] [7:34] [30:9] [35:45] [53:42]

Cycles and Orbits

Everything in creation has a particular character that gives it its special identity and outer boundaries, limitations, extent and hierarchy of connections and dependencies. Every atom, molecule, or piece of crystal broadcasts its frequency or variable vibrations in different states. Complex systems emit multitudes of vibrations and oscillating parts and are linked to each other in obvious or subtle ways.

The human body is like a microcosm that mirrors aspects of the entire macrocosm. The millions of tiny living bacteria within the human being defy accurate estimation or comprehension. The human being is like a walking mini-cosmos with countless systems and sub-systems responding to subtle means of communication. The human mind and heart has the capacity to be attuned to numerous levels of consciousness. Special insights or intuition are due to reception of special signals that are not common or usual. The less one is concerned about the material and physical, the better is the chance for insight and intuition.

The four seasons on earth and the constant changes in celestial and terrestrial cycles and orbits are manifestations of the countless variations in vibration and subtle interactions, which are often not perceptible by us. This apparent deficiency in us is a natural protection that sets outer boundaries within our human (lower) consciousness. It gives us the illusion of stability and constancy which reflects the nature of our soul and not the body and mind.

Everything within the universe fits or acts within its domain as part of the pulsating, living whole. The human soul has the capacity to resonate fully with the Master and Creator of the Cosmos. It is up to individuals to use their reasoning and intellect fully and then refer to the highest consciousness, which is the soul within the heart. The human mind and lower self are only alive due to the life force that radiates from the soul.

Whatever is in the universe or within, nature follows patterns, cycles and paths along a direction which also interacts with the wider environment and nature. The origin of the universe is the same as its final destination. In between we have an infinite variety of energies and creations.

Qur'an References: [21:33] [36:40] [13:2] [31:29] [6:2]

Planets and Stars

Stars are our heavenly companions and a source of wonder, reference and guidance. They are signs that will help us traverse the earth as well as metaphors of our inner universe. The Qur'an states that these stars and planets will help us during darkness on land and on sea. During our earthly journey we look for signs and references that help us reach our desired destinies.

The Qur'an makes an oath regarding the awesomeness of the position of stars. There is a hint in the fact that stars are receding from us yet we see them in constant positions. Then there are several references to stars collapsing upon themselves and how the sky shatters. Towards the end of creation, the stars vanish and the mountains perish and a vanishing smoke or mist prevails.

Planets are referred to as occupying the lower heavens, or what is closest to earth, and are described as beautiful decorations. The story of the solar system is that of the emergence of order from what was fiery chaos. The effect of the moon on life on earth, especially in the subtropical regions, is noticeably considerable. Historically, most travel in the desert areas was carried out at night to avoid the heat of the day. Therefore, the effect of the moon had greater impact upon life in general before the advent of urban life and mechanisation.

Our solar system is a most dynamic cosmic laboratory beset with fierce fires, ice and constant upheavals in energy and physical forms. Billions of rocks and ice orbit the sun whose core temperature is 15 million degrees centigrade. It is 150 million kilometers away from earth, over a thousand times the diameter of the earth, 330 thousand times the mass of earth – over one million earths can fit in it. The amount of energy the sun produces is billions of times more than all the electrical energy generated on earth. Man is a visiting guest in the amazing phenomena of earth, planets and stars. Outwardly we are stardust and inwardly we contain a source energy that is beyond our mental comprehension – Allah.

Qur'an References: [16:16] [37:6] [96:3] [6:97] [7:12] [56:75] [77:8] [81:2] [91:1-6] [10:5]

CHAPTER THREE

Humanity and its Journey

- Evolvement and New Emergences
- Intelligence and Consciousness
- Material Base, Spiritual Roots and Destiny
- Human Composition
- In the Womb, on Earth and in the Tomb
- The Descent and Ascent of Adam
- Provisions and Nourishment
- Information and Transformation
- Decree and Destiny
- Societies and Nations
- Cultures and Ethics
- Ancient People and their Fate
- Floods, Disasters and Destructions
- Two Stages of Life
- Recollection of Origin and End
- Higher Consciousness
- Human Nature and Self-Soul Interplay

Evolvement and New Emergences

The Qur'an declares that all human beings have been created from one self and that from that one self came its pair. All human beings are regarded as having the same potential in their spiritual capacity and their differences are mainly physical, mental and material. An outwardly poor person who has discovered inner riches may be more content and happier than an outwardly wealthy person.

There have already been numerous other creations that we do not know about which had already come and gone, either within the orbit of our universe or elsewhere. The force that propels us human beings to explore, discover and increase in knowledge is universal. Human beings are always challenged and driven towards wider and deeper levels of knowledge and consciousness. Earthly turmoil, uncertainties and difficulties are part of nature's way that drives the intelligent beings towards the higher zones of consciousness rather than to remain struggling in the cause and effect arena. Within every human being the earthly material patterns and forces meet the celestial or spiritual dimension. Balanced and wholesome life is when these two domains work in unison.

The emergence of human beings is a result of countless previous occurrences culminating with human beings as we know them. A living cell is harboured in the womb and it grows to become a clot and then a lump. After a few months the foetus enters into another phase of its emergence. At birth the human being is totally dependent upon the mother or whoever is caring for it. The Qur'an describes that after a few years, strength and determination emerge from this state of weakness, and then after a few decades weakness sets in again. The cycle of descent, ascent and descent is again completed and follows the pattern of the metaphor of Adam: From paradise to earth and then with hope and struggle back again.

Reflecting upon conception and emergence from what was not discernible has an echo in the state of timelessness. We are challenged to recall that state which is before any recollection: from the unseen to the material world and then back again to the unknown hereafter.

Qur'an References: [31:28] [3:59] [90:4] [49:18] [3:47] [2:220] [82:8] [19:67] [30:31] [36:36] [113:2] [19:9] [2:21] [30:20] [30:54] [23:11-14]

Intelligence and Consciousness

One of the greatest forces that drives the whole of creation on earth is to spread out and survive more efficiently. The innate cumulative genetic imprints and intelligence naturally favours greater levels of knowledge, strength and intelligence. Some primates may have a certain measure of awareness of themselves but it is only the human being that has full knowledge of individuality and self-awareness. The metaphor of Adam's reflections and questions in the garden highlights the rise of awareness or the rise of human intelligence and intellect.

It is through our ability to reflect, imagine and extend our mental capacity to subtler dimensions that we gain access to higher consciousness. Every healthy human being is endowed with a certain measure of self-awareness and the love of survival, strength and well-beingness. It is only when we reflect upon consciousness that is beyond personal survival and other needs that we are at the edge of the infinite vista, which is beyond the limitations of space and time. An unusual phenomenon, like a lightning bolt, is beyond the mind to comprehend and is therefore sometimes given a spiritual interpretation, because it falls beyond the realm of 'normal' consciousness. This is why it is used as a metaphor for sudden openings into higher consciousness. Out of body experiences, near death experiences, and epiphanies are not uncommon human experiences, and indicate another level of consciousness, pure consciousness or God-consciousness.

Prophetic messages and the 'sacred books' are part of human attempts to grasp higher consciousness through the application of personal discipline and will: those who begin to read and experience this new conscious map will see this life as a set of samples, metaphors and preparations for the afterlife. It is also revealed that the majority of human beings do not have the intellect, will or fortune to fully grasp this truth – this life is seen as work in progress and not everyone will understand its dynamics.

The prescription for higher consciousness is a cautious awareness at all times, the restriction of worldly distractions and desires, and maintaining the balance between the seen and the unseen, with the constant reminder that at any instant this personalised life may leave its temporary abode – the body-mind and the social nexus. God's signs on earth, including life and death and the countless cycles of movements in between, as well as matter and energy, are given to us to reflect upon so that we move beyond the mental limitations of logic and reason to experience a pure light of supreme consciousness. God-consciousness will become more constant in the hearts of those who know that the next phase of life (after death) is permanent and that one's capital in the Hereafter is totally based on appropriate intentions and actions in this world. It is for those who are constantly aware of the All-Merciful's presence and whose hearts are purified of earthly desires and attachments.

Qur'an References: [2:73] [3:118] [7:169] [21:10] [29:43] [2:63] [2:239] [50:33]

Material Base, Spiritual Roots and Destiny

The ultimate paradox in human creation relates to the mysterious connection between the material self (body, organs and elements) and the mysterious source of life which we label as soul or spirit. The success of equilibrium and fulfilment in life is based on recognising the needs of the physical side as well as the spiritual side of our makeup. Most human struggle and challenge is to reconcile this wide spectrum in our foundation.

At the physical level we are made of earthly materials with all its elements which are originally from outer space — we are made of star dust. Our soul is also a heavenly light or an energy package which beams at us a divine light with its spectrum of impulses. Our bone structure and denser aspects are earthly materials. We consist of a high content of water. Furthermore, there are considerable movements of earth, water and gas within us. Without the heat in the stomach or the firing of neurons, our life would also cease. Thus we also live by the classically recognized four principle elements: air, water, earth and fire. We need nourishment by food, water, and air as well as emotional, mental, social and spiritual fulfilment.

Generally the first third of human life is taken up by biological, physiological and mental development and growth. Then comes maturity in mind, intellect and heart. We seek knowledge and higher values as we are propelled by curiosity about the unknown. When we are in difficulty we complain and seek every possible way for resolution. Religious people call upon God or higher powers for help. Whenever we have ease we tend to forget our dependency on higher powers. Whenever we are in serious difficulties (due to our ignorance and wrong actions) we despair or get depressed. It looks as though nature itself conspires to not guarantee sustainable ease and happiness so that we seek the meaning of events as a way towards liberation and contentment. It is within human nature to act often selfishly and deny our dependence on both what is known and what is unknown. We tend to justify ourselves and argue and blame others. We are always on the edge of error and mistakes that we may regret. We are in a hurry and desire instant gratification at all times, yet we yearn for peace!

As far as our worldly endeavours are concerned we all need to exercise effort, skill and set realistic objectives. The ultimate project is however that which will enable us to understand and resonate with divine Reality. We have emanated from that zone and to it we shall return. All transient realities are dependent upon the one Supreme Reality.

Whatever we love we wish it to last forever. Love of gold is a simple example of the desire for a material that is rare and does not get tarnished. With sufficient reflection we can understand that our real nature drives us constantly towards the quality of the soul or spirit within. That spirit is a sacred reality which is deposited within our metaphorical hearts. In order to have constant reference to Allah's light we need to ensure the heart's purity so that we gain access through the light of our soul within the heart.

Qur'an References: [2:3] [3:44] [9:94] [18:26] [35:38] [36:11] [9:78] [2:245] [11:123] [10:23]

3. HUMANITY AND ITS JOURNEY

Human Composition

The soul or spirit in the children of Adam is a mysterious luminous package that is unique to human beings as it represents the highest state of consciousness. The soul which dwells within the heart is sacred; it knows boundlessness and that which is eternal. The soul reproduces all of God's higher qualities and attributes, like a living hologram emitting these lights to the human mind whilst providing life and consciousness.

Creation on earth is based on the dynamics of attraction and repulsion and the interaction of dualities and pluralities. Thus every human being is composed of the soul and its shadow companion – the self. The evolving human self or ego is like the restless shadow of the soul and yet it desires all the qualities of the soul. The real challenge to human beings is to recognise the connections between the lower self or ego and the higher self or soul, which occupies the inner heart. The lower self will discover its soul if it is groomed and disciplined towards that desirable end.

Human evolvement is both biological as well as spiritual. When full maturity is reached, then priorities may begin to change towards seeking meaning in life and higher consciousness. Success in this endeavour relates to reforming and purifying the self, thereby accessing the heart and the soul therein. Thus, the mind becomes illumined with spiritual awakening. When head and heart are in unison, spiritual maturity is attained.

The lower self is like a restless child that needs to be trained and groomed to accept boundaries and limitations. With ego restrictions there may come increased wisdom and insight. To see a situation with the least emotional or mental bias, the light of the soul becomes a guiding reference. Thus, the inner monitor is activated and thereby curbs the ego's impulsiveness and waywardness. The evolved being will realise that through faith and trust in God's presence in the heart, guidance and wholesomeness will be the order. Then one can only be in constant gratitude for the great gift of the perfect soul and God's generosity. This state of completeness is what an intelligent being aspires for.

Qur'an References: [77:20-23] [51:47-51] [7:11] [17:01] [32:07] [14:34] [16:4] [15:26] [15:29] [53:39-42] [17:13] [39:8] [41:57] [42:48] [75:14] [80:24] [86:5] [90:4] [12:87] [17:85]

In the Womb, on Earth and in the Tomb

From the infinite unseen, the universe mysteriously emerges with its countless entities and energies, all of which are interconnected. The Qur'an refers to both universal occurrence as well as human life as 'cracks' and 'openings' implying containment within space and time. Early human conception in the womb is described as a temporary settlement during which time the intrinsic shape and capacity of the foetus evolves. This temporary secure place will lead to the next temporary earthly existence where the senses and the mind begin to evolve and connect with the outer world materially and emotionally.

Our earthly life is only a prelude to another phase of creation after death. When the earth's solidity is destroyed and all matter returns to its original smoke and eventual nothingness, then every soul will experience what it had done in terms of intentions and actions on earth. The Qur'an describes this new state as a heaven and explains that the universe will return within the original sacred containment.

Like everything else in creation human life has two stages: one is normal earthly consciousness and the other is spiritual sight and awakening. Human uncertainty and concerns often stem from the innate knowledge and fear of temporariness on earth. There is a strong force within us to be secure, content and happy in a constant state rather than just the occasional pleasure of feeling good. We are driven to realise the state which recalls the garden or paradise (Adam's original inception). Our biography is that from the womb to the tomb via a short-lived time on earth, which can be either confusing or spiritually fusing. It is the fortunate one who realises the eternal truth whilst on earth (experiencing a mixture of lies and truth) before death. The hereafter and what follows in the next phase becomes smooth and easy. Otherwise, there will be periods of purification and awakening to different zones of existence towards which we are all heading.

Qur'an References: [4:126] [67:23] [3:6] [23:11-14] [32:9] [22:5] [9:118] [20:53] [40:64] [51:48] [82:4] [14:48] [39:67] [39:69]

The Descent and Ascent of Adam

The story of Adam in paradise describes a blissful state void of needs or desires. In that timeless state there was utter contentment for Adam and his complementary pair Eve. It is in that state that the soul or spirit of Adam carries the 'Knowledge' to which the earthling human descendants aspire. The Qur'an describes how Satan whispers to Adam that suggest if he desires eternal life then he can guide him to that. Then the voice of truth warns Adam and his offspring not to be infatuated by Satan who had managed to banish Adam from his perfect abode. Those who believe in God and His perfect ways and eternal presence will avoid the pitfalls of Satan. Those who do not live by this faith may succumb to illusions and fancy desires, which can only lead to utter loss and destruction.

The descent of Adam is towards the earthly life where there is duality, opposition, enmity and all kinds of forces and powers that cause misery, fear and unhappiness. The Qur'an unequivocally tells us that some of us will be enemies of others. Human beings are also forgetful and weak in their resolve. For contemplative beings it is the realisation of truth and arrival at truth that becomes the driving force for liberation. Whoever is in self-awareness and does not follow the whims of the lower self or the ego is on the path that will lead back to the garden of contentment. Even when such a being attains the state of the garden they still pray to their Lord to complete their light, which is absolute perfection without any discernible or created 'entities' such as the garden. Whenever such beings experience the wonderment of Paradise they even recall that they tasted a similar state on earth.

Human life on earth is naturally full of challenges and choices that can either make us more base and materially chained or drive us more towards higher levels of consciousness. Our earthly life could be the springboard back to the state of inner bliss.

The rise of the Adamic consciousness, with its subtle neuron web in the brain and mental processes accompanied by a sense of separation and inquisitiveness, necessitated the descent to the earthly zone of experience in order to ultimately taste transcendence. This new cradle of mankind is the base of evolution from the one cell towards the most complex human being.

Every human being goes through a physical process of growing from a cell to a clot to a foetus, and then once born, into a growing baby. Upon maturity the quest for security and happiness becomes the dominant drive in life. Adam now desires a return to eternal paradise and its perfections.

The cycles of birth and death are echoed in the descent of Adam and the ascent back to pure consciousness. The living emanates from the dead and the dead from the living and this paradox cannot be resolved rationally. It may dissolve through insight and illumination the keys to which are faith in God and transcending to truth.

Qur'an References: [20:120-121] [21:34] [4:1] [7:27] [2:36] [7:26] [17:70] [7:172] [20:115] [2:35] [46:14] [47:6] [79:41] [19:61] [66:8] [2:25]

Provisions and Nourishment

Life on earth is work in progress. Everything had emerged from the unseen to interact, connect and move along its destiny back to the unseen: from Allah, to Allah, and by Allah. Whatever is living on earth grows to a certain level of its potential and consciousness and is already defined by the innate soul or spirit of the creature. During that process it draws energy and nourishment from what is visible and also from what is subtle and imperceptible. Plants synthesise their own nourishment through sun, water and chlorophyll. Others draw their nourishment from those that are lower in the food chain, as well as energy, heat and light. The Qur'an declares that whatever is on earth is for the use of human beings in their journey. Man, who is endowed with the potential of being a steward or custodian on earth, is also given the responsibility to be frugal, just and non-wasteful. If all that is on earth was created for man, then man was created to realise the Supreme creator and abide by His will.

We are reminded that our stay on earth is temporary and short. If we are not careful and responsible it could also be brutal and dreadful. The lower tendencies in human beings which bring about arrogance, distractions and disasters are a common cause for 'hell'. Constant reminders as to the purpose of life can bring about clarity and strength along the journey. The Prophets have relied upon the Creator for guidance towards achieving a personal and collective goodly life. We are constantly warned not to be unjust with our powers and wealth. The prescription is to struggle in the way of higher knowledge and transformation with all of the provisions that we have – our time and wealth. Those who spend generously, openly and secretly, will certainly reap their reward on earth as well as the hereafter.

We are all warned that all earthly possessions are transitory and what will remain is the state of the heart and spiritual evolvement. Ultimately all provisions and nourishments are for awakening to the inner truth and to realise that life on earth is only a prelude to a next phase. It is a wise being who is not envious of those who have much wealth and power on earth. He knows that all worldly engagements are accompanied by distractions and regrets except for what is necessary for inner growth.

The next phase of life is such that no amount of wealth on this earth would be of any use and such advantages do not help us to realise the eternal truth within the soul. In the next phase of life all that we have as our capital is purity at heart. Reflection and accountability in this life will help focus upon intention, action and self-awareness. It is the intelligent person who knows that all experiential states are temporary and it is God-consciousness that enables an easy transition to the hereafter.

Qur'an References: [2:60] [20:131] [28:82] [34:4] [45:5] [3:37] [22:58] [29:17] [51:22]

Information and Transformation

The link between the lower and higher self is through sense, mind, intellect and insight of the heart. Our senses connect us to the outer world and are coordinated through the inner sense that feeds into the faculty of imagination, reflection and thinking – the mind. We are naturally inquisitive and curious, and desire to acquire more knowledge and information, much of which is useful for day-to-day existence and survival.

Information that impacts upon our thoughts and actions is a seed of transformation, according to the extent of the impact upon one's life. An event or information may arouse curiosity or instigate desires, whilst others may alarm or arouse emotions, fears or anger. Outer information and experiences may bring about a rise in consciousness and some measure of transcendence of a different nature to normal everyday consciousness. All information or knowledge is an opportunity for a shift in consciousness.

Generally, information gives us some idea or knowledge about an outer situation and its relationship with one's personal views and needs. We often know through self-awareness when we act arrogantly or selfishly, and it is only when knowledge is internalised and has become a part of one's mental reference that transformation begins. Self-awareness and constant reference to a desirable state can speed up spiritual growth.

Transformed beings see with eyes and insights, and hear with ears as well as their hearts. This state becomes like a torchlight in one's hand along the dark and treacherous earthly pathways.

Qur'an References: [2:36] [2:185] [56:73] [26:79] [80:24-32] [18:46] [26:88] [104:3] [57:20] [4:29] [61:11] [2:274] [9:85] [70:24] [2:29]

Decree and Destiny

All energies and existing entities follow certain patterns and measures according to different qualities and quantities. Countless energies and entities interact with each other producing new situations which are more complex than before. In our investigative endeavour we look at creation from numerous angles such as the physical, the chemical, the biological, mathematical, social and other viewpoints and knowledges. Every entity in existence follows one or more pattern and design. There are countless laws and paths; some are known while others are not known and therefore need exploring to be understood. Our physical world is a stepping stone towards the vast world of the unseen. The human psyche is a natural bridge between the physical and the spiritual. We are subject to the universal laws that govern other creation, terrestrial and celestial.

Decrees represent laws and patterns that govern life. Destiny is the personal experience that is the result of interacting with natural laws which operate within our human systems as well as in the outer world. We are constantly challenged in this life and face uncertainties and obstacles. Yet we desire ease and wholesome outcomes at all times. What we experience at any moment is a result of our past intentions and actions and the relationships with the outer world. The outcome of these interactive forces is what an individual experiences both physically and mentally.

The material world, as well as our mental state, is subject to constant change and we realise these changes because we have within us a stable and constant soul or spirit. The more one is in touch with this inner soul at all times, the more likely the outcome of our inner state will be acceptable. 'Good' destinies are the product of appropriate intentions, good attention and efficient action. The more our intentions are oriented towards a higher cause or consciousness, the more likely that our experiences will continue to be of greater desirability.

All the laws that govern the universe and the energy fields of 'good' and 'bad' can be likened to clouds in cyberspace. Appropriate spiritual upbringing is to do with how we tune ourselves to these energy fields to avoid the usual human dramas of misery and difficulty. A healthy individual interacts with the world by bringing about both outer change as well as inner adaptation.

Human development begins with attention and care to the lower self and issues of survival and selfishness. With maturity and better understanding of the nature of the self, one acts in a more balanced and just way. Fairness, self-awareness and concern for others are key entry points to the zone of soul referencing and connection between mind and heart. Pursuance of short term pleasures and self-gratification will always lead to disappointments. Serving others and purifying the heart from anger, hatred and other vices are the steps that may lead to salvation from the shadowy lower self and the recognition of the soul whose nature is perfect and eternal. This realisation leads us to a wholesome destiny.

Qur'an References: [7:25] [2:20] [5:19] [35;44] [13.8] [66:8] [64:1] [2:210] [10:54] [41:45]

Societies and Nations

Modern human beings have emerged from one blueprint some two hundred thousand years ago. During the past hundred thousand years there have been numerous waves of homo sapiens radiating out of Asia, Africa, the Mediterranean basin and further afield. These small bands of people had lived very precariously and while some of them flourished and grew more in numbers, others died out.

Food and safety were key factors for survival. For that reason, migrating human beings who were near rivers, lakes and oceans probably had an easier time. Each group would have probably had a natural leader who was endowed with physical and/or mental strength. Shamans and other seers were also amongst early leaders from both sexes. After many thousands of years of hunting and gathering, foraging and herding followed. Then came early agricultural settlements some ten thousand years ago. Then chiefs and priests began to regulate life and messengers and prophets appeared. The insight and intuitive capacity of these early prophets must have helped these small societies to be peaceful and relatively stable. The flood of Noah may be a marking point between the era of instability of people and that which came later, which was more governed and regulated by better rulers and laws.

Different cultures and people had their special habits and social norms which suited their way of life and the environment. Geography and the extent of reliance on agriculture were hallmarks of the religious cultures. Differences in language, race, ethnicity and gender issues were taken into consideration by the different religious paths. We can now look at these different religions with the advantage of our analytical tools and discover that there was a unifying thread between most of them and that differences were mainly related to the specific context of the time and place.

From around five thousand years ago we have the emergence of Chiefs, Kings and the Priestly caste reinforcing each other. In some cases the Priests were very much involved in regulating the affairs of the people. In Egypt they were responsible for measuring the Nile's level in order to assess appropriate taxation to be extracted from the peasants.

About a thousand years ago we could have counted many thousands of different languages, cultures and religions. With increased connections and communication worldwide, greater uniformity will no doubt reduce cultural and linguistic differences. It is now estimated that a language dies out every couple of weeks. Also, because of environmental degradation many species of creatures die out all the time.

It is a human duty to ensure minimal disturbance on earth. Yet human beings are the biggest perpetrators of extinctions. Although every human soul is the same in essence, outer differences of colour, shape and culture are part of the inherited natural diversity of humanity.

Qur'an References: [49:13] [29:2] [3:7] [2:143] [13:30] [3:110] [7:34] [16:36] [16:93] [45:28]

Cultures and Ethics

Cultures and languages evolved as human beings spread throughout the earth and settled in fertile lands in clusters of clans and communities. Seers, shamans, prophets and messengers arose from amongst these different peoples to explain the purpose of life and God's will and governance. Seafaring people were shown aspects of God's presence differently to land-based, agricultural settlements. God's ways in creation were described as meaningful to the specific culture and way of life of the people. Religious ideas, teachings and rituals had a strong geographical and cultural colour.

What all of the prophets, messengers, apostles and sages have in common is their surrendering to truth, living through God-consciousness, and thereby acting justly with no regrets or sorrows. Differences in language, race, ethnicity and gender are seen as outer shells and temporary, as everything will totally disappear in the hereafter. The real difference between the children of Adam is the extent of their resonance with Divine guidance and inspiration. There is a clear, unifying thread in the messages of all prophets, with different emphasis due to the historical and cultural context of their time.

The prophets' main role was to bring justice to their people and accountability for everyone, individually as well as collectively. The prophets' conduct evokes God's unity and reflects that the quality of life is in accordance with faith and trust in God's perfect ways. They all warned against arrogance, pride, and oppression of the weak and the poor. Generosity, charity and good conduct are a main feature of these messages. All goodness emanates from Allah – the most generous, forgiving, loving, majestic, and the source of all beauty, harmony and peace. It is the human duty to reflect some of these Divine attributes on earth and take on Allah's colours, individually and collectively.

Qur'an References: [2:213] [10:19] [22:40]

3. HUMANITY AND ITS JOURNEY

Ancient People and their Fate

Numerous prophets and messengers have helped man understand the map of life and how to resonate with it. The earliest named prophet is Adam, then Noah, then Abraham, and then others with considerable detail – especially Moses. Several nations and people who had lived in Arabia had not followed their prophets and the end result was doom and disaster.

The flood of Noah caused the complete destruction of the land and its people. The prophet Hud had warned his people (called 'Aad) without success until they were overtaken by fierce storms (cyclones or tornados) that lasted seven nights and eight days. Then we have the story of people of Thamud who had persisted in demanding a miracle from their Prophet Saleh. This miracle was the emergence of a she-camel which had to be given its share of water. Again these people denied the she-camel her share of provision and she was slaughtered. They too were caught by natural disaster (earthquake) which immobilized them for three consecutive days. The Prophet Shu'aib, near the modern town of 'Aqaba, had also been warning his people with reminders of what came to the people of Noah, Hud and Thamud. Where he lived in Madyan has been excavated more recently.

We have the stories of the Prophet Abraham and his journey from Ur, in southern modern-day Iraq up north to Haraan (modern Turkey) and then down to Palestine and Egypt. Angels appeared to him to announce that he would have offspring even though he was over 100 years old. His nephew Lot had angels visiting him as a warning against the wrongdoing of his people.

As for the story of Moses, it appears in the Qur'an extensively, spread out over 35 chapters. He too managed to save his clan from the oppression of an Egyptian Pharaoh through a miraculous parting of the sea on to Sinai. He had already crossed the Sinai desert before seeking enlightenment and guidance. The Prophet Joseph, who was the ancestor of the Israelites in Egypt, fulfilled a prophecy of a dream he had where he would become a ruler of a land.

Most of the people and Prophets mentioned in Qur'an were naturally from areas known to the Arabs and the merchants of Makkah and Madinah. No people are left without some guidance regarding their purpose and direction in life. The majority of denials and lack of faith is attributed to habits of the past and the objectors' claim that the way of their ancestors was the best and thus they adhered to it. It is a natural tendency in human beings to follow the familiar, especially when it comes to issues of survival, or comfort and ease.

Qur'an References: [13:22] [13:35] [3:137] [11:49] [12:109] [27:51] [28:83] [35:44]

3. HUMANITY AND ITS JOURNEY

Floods, Disasters and Destruction

Life on earth is a work in progress with regards to human beings and natural evolution. There are several levels of human nature. At the base there is a material, physical and biological structure. Then we have the layers of emotional and mental nature. We also need social and cultural links. There is also a constant yearning for discovery of meaning and a spiritual life. Human nature is like a spectrum that spans a very wide range of colours, hues and states.

The Qur'an mentions earth or clay as the foundational base of the human form, whereas the soul or spirit is the source of life that drives humankind. This soul is sacred for it is the divine spirit which was blown into Adam, causing all the angels to prostrate to him.

Through an evolving consciousness, a contemplative person will realise that needs, desires and attachments are part of human nature. The spiritual aspiration to transcend these limitations is also a major drive in life. Followers of great prophets and messengers who had experienced high levels of consciousness rose beyond personal and social limitations to taste an inner state of joy that was beyond any describable happiness or pleasure.

Spiritual evolvement implies moving along a path of conduct that enables one to access more frequently the divine light emitted by the soul through the purified heart. Most religious doctrines prescribe appropriate conduct and maintaining purity at heart as a means for spiritual advancement. Life is the battlefield between the lower and the higher within us. And it is only by God-consciousness and grace that we are able to be clear in our choices, direction and boundaries. For some people the self-soul interplay is like a child's game and they move swiftly to soul-realisation and contentment on earth. For others it may be a prolonged battle, even a losing one.

To have had a healthy upbringing and a good religion does not in any way guarantee a goodly life and happiness. Human beings are the 'middle people' between the most sublime and the ridiculous, or the dreadful and confused. We have a certain impulse to leave illusion and fantasy behind and realise the perfection of the soul within. This self-awareness will illumine our life and bring about access to inner joy irrespective of outer circumstances.

Qur'an References: [4:13] [64:11] [27:69]

Two Stages of life

The message of Islam and the Qur'an highlight the two phases of human life: one being earthly and therefore transitory, the other being life after death. Our life on earth is where we can be prepared with better understanding and be equipped for life after death when we lose all power, will or ability to act or change anything. Our life after death follows according to our state of consciousness and spiritual realisation at the point of death. In this life we are subject to the direction of time and limitations of space. After death, and especially after resurrection, we enter into a zone where space seems infinite and so does time.

Some people cannot accept this map of two stages of life and therefore concentrate all their efforts on worldly gain, such as power, knowledge, or simply comfort and ease. For these people there will be a bleak life after death for they have not been prepared to cope with the entirely new zone of existence. It is like a foetus in the womb that denies the future use or need of eyes, ears or limbs which are vital for the experience of life after birth. The majority of people are considered to be limited in their consciousness and are totally concerned and attached to the physical world and their concerns about it. There are others who deny this world and are mostly concerned about the hereafter.

The Qur'an advocates the middle path and the use of human experience and knowledge in this world as a prelude to the next. The people of the middle way know that one cannot entirely control worldly experiences, for they are always subject to change. There is a relief when we realise that beneath all our endeavours what we are all aspiring for is wellbeing and contentment in body, mind and heart. In truth, joy and happiness always reside in the heart and access to that is potentially possible for all mankind.

Our earthly life is shown to be a metaphor: how rain and sun bring to life herbage and animals on earth and then through natural change we find that where there had once been forests teeming with life barren desert now remains. The Qur'an advocates reflection upon the nature of our life on earth. We are warned against attachment to worldly possessions and powers and that from our own close relatives and family we may experience enmity and difficulty. We are also told that it is natural for human beings to be weak and to prefer not to think of the hereafter but only dwell upon what our minds and lower nature demands for survival. The quest for arrival is often postponed because of the day to day 'needs' as perceived by the agitated mind.

Qur'an References: [2:86] [2:200-201] [3:56] [3:152] [7:32] [9:38] [9:69] [18:45] [10:24] [10:64] [13:26] [18:46] [29:64] [41:31] [87:16]

Recollection of Origin and End

It is in our nature to be curious about our world and search for reasons and meanings. The toddler explores his immediate environment and the mature person wonders what there is beyond the oceans or in the heavens. It is also natural for most human beings to be curious about their lineage and genealogy. The impulse to look for one's roots and ancestors and beyond is deeply ingrained in us and it may even be that we are wired genetically in this quest. We often ask each other what is the earliest memory we have and some forms of healing even try to wipe out the trauma of emerging through the birth canal from the subconscious.

Mind, memory and intellect develop as the brain stabilises and grows in its complex capacity. Naturally we also forget what is often not conducive to our lives. The desire for a good memory is also natural in us, especially as we grow older and our mental functions slow down. With old age, however, the quality and relevance of what is being considered may be enhanced. Then there is another type of recollection which is akin to intuition or insight. It is through this 'hidden' consciousness that we can realise our position on earth as being bracketed between birth and death and that our desire for longevity or a better understanding of eternity is more to do with the nature of our soul than our earthly limitations.

The intuitive quality and spiritual reflection does relate to the extent of our faith and our belief in the nature of the soul and its ongoingness after death. We naturally resent constrictions and difficulties on earth, which are all part of our lower nature, but these can be an incentive to seek expansion and greater horizons in a meaning sense rather than material. Remembrance of God, prayers and access to higher consciousness are steps which may enable us to rise above worldly limitations and have greater insights regarding our sublime origin and return to it.

The Qur'an provides numerous verses showing the map of proper reflection and remembrance of God – who is ever-present and closer than our jugular vein – that sublime presence is not subject to any distance. We are also reminded that everyone is afflicted with goodness and difficulty in order for us to declare our incapacity to control our material or mental outcome so that we refer back to our origins – Allah.

Qur'an References: [74:55] [2:152] [19:67] [37:13] [18:24] [2:231] [7:69] [8:2] [51:55] [7:57] [2:221] [14:25] [28:46] [3:7] [6:126] [7:130] [13:28] [58:19] [29:45] [72:17] [33:41] [50:8] [87:9] [76:1] [7:168] [96:8] [53:52] [70:39] [96:14]

Higher Consciousness

Basic self-awareness is the natural state of a healthy human being. Self-awareness can evolve to higher states of consciousness. Life begins as a basic self-propagating occurrence and leads to human self-awareness, as well as being aware of the environment at the same time. The basic natural drive for self-preservation and survival have led human beings to the constant enquiry and desire to know what is behind all limiting factors on earthly life. We have long been relentlessly exploring the constituents of an atom and the furthest of stars and galaxies. Philosophers, psychologists and religiously-oriented people have also been constantly probing the nature of the human self, its boundaries, origin and destination.

An intelligent teenager wonders who he or she really is. The early periods of human growth is much involved with developing the physical and material aspects of our nature. With maturity, balanced hormones, and diverse experiences in life, many a questioning person will interrogate subtle aspects of life and living. With religious practices and other related paths of self-knowledge, the idea of higher consciousness, God-consciousness, or enlightenment becomes an objective to be studied or perhaps attained.

The Qur'an prescribes a path of cautious awareness and constant referencing to remembrance of God and higher consciousness. People on this path emerge from darkness to light, until they realise that the entire universe is permeated by a sacred light that is beyond the boundaries of understanding by the human mind. People on this path would also recognise the numerous degrees and levels of subtler and higher consciousness. This sort of knowledge begins with discernible and teachable factual information and leads towards higher inner knowledge and transformation. At that point sublime consciousness, perfect beauty, light of knowledge, absolute ability, universal sight and all other great attributes meet and unify in the oneness of Supreme Consciousness.

For a spiritual seeker the journey in this life represents a constant movement from the more material realm towards the subtle zone of the unseen that lies beyond our comprehension. It is a journey which begins with self-awareness and ends with soul-realisation. That is the real purpose and path of liberation from all limitations.

Qur'an References: [64:3] [5:93] [29:49] [16:97] [19:60] [2:82] [11:23] [65:11] [66:8] [6:83] [20:75] [58:11] [30:8] [55:38] [72:26]

Human Nature and Self-Soul Interplay

Our life's experiences on earth are all bifurcated into dualities, opposites and complementarities. Our knowledge and understanding in life is always enhanced through symbols, metaphors and examples. If there is no honey to taste we can use dates or sugar to give an idea of the sweetness of honey. The human capacity for referencing and putting things in context is unique to our mental capacity and consciousness.

The Qur'an is described as giving examples of every possible thing in existence so that we may reflect upon these and remember their origin. We are given numerous descriptions of what is considered real on earth, but are also reminded that all of these realities are transient and have their roots and origin in one sacred Reality to which they all return – Allah. Life on this earth is like the example of a person who has lit a fire in order to see and understand what is around him. Once the fire is alight then it begins to subside and disappear. The person is back again in darkness. Also the example is given of rain from heavens bringing herbage and life upon earth. A time will come where forests and gardens will become sand dunes.

The human journey on earth is like these examples. We emerge ignorant and grow in our mental capacity and physical ability and eventually attain some wisdom and insight. The cycle begins with weakness and ends up with some outer weakness. But if inner realisation and awakening to the eternal truth had been attained then all is well. The Qur'an repeatedly reminds us that all of these signs, symbols and metaphors are for us to reflect upon so that we realise the constant truth of divine presence as a foundation for all transience and change. The Qur'an also describes that those who recognise this truth are indeed those who are endowed with spiritual knowledge, the biggest gift and grace.

Liberating human beings from personal, mental and social veils is like freeing a slave who is owned by several quarrelsome masters. Every instant there are conflicting instructions and demands by an incompetent person who is incapable of any progress. The contrast is the liberated person who has a clear idea of the destination and the code of conduct (the Deen) along this path. We are also given the example of how great beings such as prophets were close to their enemies. The example of the Prophets Lot and Noah and their wives is given. The reverse is also true: that of a greater despotic Pharaoh (probably Ramses the 2nd) and his most righteous wife Asiya who suffered from him. The Qur'an reminds us that the ultimate metaphor is the human self itself. It contains the best of the best (the sacred soul) and the worst of the worst (the lower ego-self).

An intelligent, reflective person will realise that we need to be clear about personal will and responsibility before applying and living the prophetic path. During our lifetime, no doubt we will come across obstacles, difficulties and distractions. These forces can strengthen the resolve of those who are steadfast and in constant remembrance, or cause distraction and loss for those weak in faith and application.

Qur'an References: [29:43] [18:56] [10:24] [14:25] [39:27] [2:17] [2:261] [3:59] [11:24] [29:41] [62:5] [16:75] [39:29] [66:10-11] [64:1] [39:67] [11:118] [9:32] [18:9] [74:31] [6:59]

CHAPTER FOUR

Wisdom, God-Consciousness and Revelations

- Witnessing, Insights and Revelations
- Sacred Expressions and Books
- All Within Sacred Grace
- The 'Adamic Blueprint'
- Religions and Cultures
- Faith and Denials
- Will to Realise Unity
- Knowledge and Ignorance
- Friends of Allah
- Recollection and Awakening
- Middle People
- Perfecting Worship – the Deen of Islam
- Liberating Intentions and Actions

Witnessing, Insights and Revelations

It is natural for us to have our senses sharp and clear in order to reflect the outer world as accurately as possible. The most frequent metaphors used in the Qur'an are those of having sight or being blind or deaf or hearing clearly. We are handicapped if the senses or the brain that processes and stores experiences are not functioning efficiently. The Qur'an asserts that those who are blind in this world (who do not understand things rationally and sensibly) will be blind in the next world and even more confused. This world is indeed a necessary preparation and foundation for the next.

Physical blindness or other handicaps can be of hindrance to a certain extent but there are some compensations. In old Arabic cultures the person who was born blind was often named 'the seer', who sees better in an inner sense. Clarity, sights and insights are often considered as a gift to those who live their Deen and are committed to striving towards better deeds and a selfless way of life. Real blindness is defined as that of the heart within the breast. The metaphorical heart is considered as the home of the sacred soul or spirit which every human being has been given as the ultimate grace from Allah.

The highest levels of inspiration are labelled as revelation or sublime sacred communication. Moses was inspired through revelation to hit the sea with his walking stick in order to cross it. The Prophet is like everyone else with the exception of receiving clear revelation. This unusual gift had caused the Prophet Noah to warn his people of impending doom. It is said by the Prophet Muhammad that there were 124,000 beings who had come to humanity as prophets with the message of the Truth of Oneness that encompasses the universe, and towards which human beings need to focus and connect with by will and deeds.

When the Qur'an reminds us to reflect upon those who are physically deaf or blind, it is for us to see the parallel regarding insights and inner hearing of subtler meanings in life. The parable that is often drawn is that of darkness and light. A dead person cries in anguish, 'Why am I blind in this realm (in the hereafter) if I had good sight on earth?'

The faculty of insight and deeper understanding has to be developed through personal will and discipline. Accepting outer boundaries and ethical conduct whilst pursuing selfless actions that increase compassion and empathy are essential grounds for spiritual growth and insights.

4. WISDOM, GOD-CONSCIOUSNESS & REVELATIONS

There are numerous levels of insight and wisdom which lead ultimately to what is described as revelations, which can pick up aspects of the ancient past as well as the future. Our life on earth is a metaphor of the unseen world or the hereafter, and our faculties of sight, hearing and understanding are samples of what will become clearer later after death.

Qur'an References: [6:104] [22:46] [6:50] [13:16] [17:72] [20:125] [40:58] [17:39] [4:163] [26:63] [3:44] [39:65] [38:70]

Sacred Expressions and Books

In the history of prophets and messengers, many have been accused of being mad. Their warnings and messages were naturally unusual and often unacceptable to their people, thus resulting in this type of accusation. These beings were experiencing life through the laws of higher consciousness and therefore saw outer differences and dualities as veils and barriers from the one cosmic source from which they have emerged and to which they are returning. They realised the immense power of the present moment which contains in essence all that is within time and space. Their warnings were stern and their good news gave joy to the few who believed the message and followed the prescribed path of conduct in life.

Truth is sacred, timeless and prevails universally. A sacred expression is an attempt to describe an immense reality that is constant and universally dominant. A sacred book is a comprehensive unveiling of the meaning of life and the prescriptions to evolve to its promise. The Qur'an is described as a book of immense sacredness that can only be approached with utter humility and purity at heart. It is like a shaft of light that descends from upper heavens, so that we connect the visible world with its origin.

Twenty-six prophets and messengers were specifically mentioned in the Qur'an as they were relevant or known to the Arabian people. The Prophet Muhammad said that there had been 124,000 messengers. In a broader sense every entity in existence expresses its innate nature and thereby reveals its reality in that message. Whatever there is in the universe declares its natural tendency and its destiny. For human beings who possess a wide spectrum of consciousness and possible behaviour and action, a revealed message gives much insight and guidance for a good future on earth as well as in the hereafter.

Countless realities have emerged from one Reality and are returning to it. Prescriptions are given to us so that we fully understand and experience the mystery of divine Oneness. Warnings and good news always come together and that is one of the meanings of the expression 'human beings are the middle people'. We are between the seen and the unseen, repulsion and acceptance, virtues and vices, birth and death.

Qur'an References: [76:23] [62:2] [56:77-87] [2:151] [05:83] [25:7] [26:62] [33:40] [46:35] [62:2] [68:46] [90:11-16] [107:123]

All Within Sacred Grace

The great mystery of the beginning of creation and its amazing rapidity of development and evolvement is a prelude to the greater mystery of the all-pervading Oneness that envelops the immense diversity and differences in creations. The Divine Presence encompasses what is in the heavens and earth and is present within the human heart as a soul. Thus, Allah's light and consciousness is the whole of creation at all times. The challenge to human beings in this life is to realise that Allah is the Master of the Universe and the sole Lord and Owner of what is known and unknown.

This Divine light is the source of life and consciousness. Every entity that has awareness and sentiency experiences an aspect of life and is energised by different levels of consciousness. Human beings are gifted with the highest levels of awareness and the widest spectrum of life's experiences, from the physical to the most subtle, from emotions to moral values that lead to God-consciousness and enlightenment. The way to know Allah and His way is through self-knowledge. Human beings can easily understand the ever-changing lower self and, by transcending the ego, can witness the Divine Attributes and lights through the soul.

In the light of such awesome beauty and majesty the believer is humbled to submit to this amazing truth and reality that there is only the Divine Being in existence. In so doing, the enlightened being gains access to the original abode of Adam – the state of paradise – within the heart. Wherever one is, God is there, and whenever one reflects, God is the source and cause of that reflection. He is the First before any beginning and the Last beyond every end. The mind cannot comprehend the Truth of divine nature; only through a purified heart does the real unveiling begin to unfold and completely take over all veils and shadows of what appears as 'other' than the One.

Qur'an References: [64:8] [5:48] [3:179] [3:44] [50:45] [53:13] [6:103] [57:3] [41:21]

The 'Adamic Blueprint'

The universe contains countless types of energy and matter that are permeated by the original light and essence of God. The human soul is a special sacred package of energy that is lodged within the human heart, which is independent of the death of the body.

Like the Divine Light, the soul is not subject to cycles of change or reductions. Allah is the only one unique Reality, which is self-sustaining and is not subject to any change. His light is incomparable, eternal and ever-present at all times and everywhere. From it, space and time have manifested to contain earthly experiences. Human spiritual evolvement implies awareness and consciousness of the ever–present dominance and governance of Allah. Thus, it is natural wisdom to submit, yield to and accept this perfect truth. This is the purpose of human life on earth.

The story of Adam in paradise and his curiosity as to the state of eternity signifies the rise of personal conditioned consciousness, and apparent separation from Reality. Then Adam (his soul) was given the knowledge of Allah's Attributes: life, power, knowledge, ability, will and others. It is through these that separation is bridged and unity is established. By grooming the lower self and yielding to the supremacy of the soul, Adam's offspring can access paradise within. Passion for paradise can drive us to rediscover its state and thereby attain liberation from earthly exile and limitations.

We grow mentally and intellectually by exercising reason and wisdom. With faith and constant religious and spiritual practices, we begin to experience the realms beyond earthly dualities and causalities that lie at the shore of the boundless ocean of incomparability, whilst still perched on the shifting sands of relativities.

The soul or spirit that lies within the heart of the children of Adam is a mysterious package that is unique to human beings. It represents the ultimate divine gift as it resonates with all the great qualities of Allah – like a living hologram. The human being is composed of the soul and its shadow companion – the self. The human self or ego is like the restless shadow of the soul and it desires all the qualities that reside within the soul. The real challenge to human beings is to recognise the connections between the lower self or ego and the higher self or soul, and thus work to groom the self and make it under the soul's power.

Qur'an References: [12:53] [15:29] [17:85] [91:7-10] [20:115] [32:7] [84:6] [4:113] [91:7-10]

Religions and Cultures

Religions have evolved into systems of belief and conduct that help to regulate people's lives, to enable them to gain goodness and happiness and to attain durability and lasting benefits for all. Cultures are often coupled with religion and other communal ideas including status, power, habits in everyday life and other factors which produce distinct behaviours and tendencies.

Islam is based upon the Qur'an and the teachings and conduct of the Prophet Muhammad. It also acknowledges the Abrahamic prophets and a few others. The Prophet Muhammad had said that there were many thousands of prophets but the Qur'an mentions the following names (in Arabic with the English equivalent):

Adam*	Adam	Lut	Lot
Al-Yasa	Elisha	Musa*	Moses
Ayyub	Job	Muhammad	
Dawud	David	Nuh	Noah
Harun	Aaron	Saleh	Salih
Hizqil	Ezekiel	Shu'ayb	Jethro
Hud	Eber/Heber	Sulayman*	Solomon
Ibrahim*	Abraham	Uzair	Ezra
Idris	Enoch	Yahya	John
Ilyas	Elias	Ya'qub	Jacob
Isa*	Jesus	Yunus	Jonah
Ishaq	Isaac	Yusuf	Joseph
Ismail	Ishmael	Zakariyah	Zachariah

*Traditionally in Islam, these five prophets are referred to as the 'Resolute Messengers'.

The Qur'an declares that the essence of the messages of the prophets was the same – declaring God's unity and Lordship over all of creation. The prophets spread the message that the purpose of human life is to submit to God's perfect will and live on earth in preparation for the hereafter. Outer differences between prophets are due to the time and culture of their people.

The Qur'an dwells mostly upon Abraham's lineage and prophets that were relevant to the Arabs and the people in the Middle East and the Mediterranean region.

The Prophets Noah, Abraham, Moses and numerous others before Jesus have all declared that there is One Sublime God who had created the universe and that human beings should submit to this truth and practice transformative worship in preparation for the hereafter. Over thousands of years these enlightened beings disclosed what was revealed to them about the sacred light and its presence throughout the universe. They spoke the language of their people and addressed worldly issues relevant to their cultures, highlighting the purpose of man and the privilege of stewardship and its responsibility towards all creation.

The prophets mentioned in the Qur'an represent a small portion of many others who came to other people and cultures in ancient times, giving warnings as well as the good news. Good deeds and awareness of the hereafter, hell and paradise and resurrection was a central message of all these prophets. Life on earth is a testing ground in preparation for the eternal state after death. These prophets are considered a brotherhood in enlightenment, following in the footsteps of the ancient ones like Noah and Abraham.

Qur'an References: [3:194] [4:164-165] [6:42] [8:56] [3:64] [5:32] [9:128] [14:04] [23:32]

4. WISDOM, GOD-CONSCIOUSNESS & REVELATIONS

Faith and Denials

The number and types of seekers of truth (individuals and groups), their religions, culture and racial background are numerous and complex but their desired destination is similar.

Human beings seek a destiny of durable contentment, peace and happiness. The path to this end is that of submission (Islām) to the innate driving force of faith (Imān) in God's generosity, mercy and forgiveness. We need to maintain great caution (taqwa) from the dangers of outer distractions in order to be attuned to higher consciousness and awareness of Divine presence and dominance. The perfection of this transformation is faultless and leads to the ultimate transaction (Ihsān) – total awareness of God's presence and guidance to pure consciousness that supersedes but does not obliterate other levels of awareness of experience.

Prophets have taught that he who knows himself knows his Lord. Self-knowledge is, therefore, the foundation of spiritual progress and evolvement. The human soul belongs to the realm of subtle entities and lights. It is a Divine entity, energised by the spirit (rūh) while interacting with physical matter, the mind and the changing self. The human soul provides the body and mind with life, whereas its root and essence is the Divine spirit. The human position on earth is the bridge and interspace between this world and the world of the unseen beyond the limitations of space and time. As our essential nature is spiritual light, we yearn constantly for the perfect and boundless realm of absolute goodness and perfection – paradise. We often resent our temporary exile on earth due to the soul's memory of the eternal garden.

It is essential for the seeker of self-knowledge to practice modesty, courage, wisdom and justice. When the lower self is groomed and the natural, early vices of the ego have been checked and replaced with virtues, the new habits will drive the person towards higher attributes which reside in the heart and are emitted by the soul. The ultimate religious, spiritual or moral grooming is to purify the heart so that the lights of the soul can shine through. When the lower self has been curbed and harnessed, the soul will simply reflect the essential qualities of generosity, mercy, forbearance, forgiveness, modesty, patience, knowledge and natural wholesomeness. When the vices of the ego yield to the virtues of the soul, a delightful unison and contentment takes place – sustainable joy.

Faith and trust in the all-Merciful God are required for proper understanding and absorption of the message of Qur'anic revelation. This Book of treasures will only have an impact upon those whose hearts are ready to be illumined. The light of the Qur'an is barred from the sceptics and those in denial of the One God.

Many of the Qur'anic messages and revelations have several levels of meanings and depths. Most Arabic-speaking people can understand the basic linguistic meaning, while a deeper understanding can touch seekers of truth and a yet deeper impact awaits those who are absorbed in a life of religious observation and conduct. With a purified, believing heart, the listener can resonate with the insights and wisdom of the revelations.

Only the purified heart can be guided by faith towards higher levels of spiritual awareness and sensitivity until a level of certainty is reached that brings about God-consciousness at all times.

Whoever believes in Allah's purpose and will and acts for the good of mankind and the rest of creation will progress along the spiritual path. Faith and Islam is followed by leaving behind old ways, habits and sometimes even home and family. The struggle towards improving one's inner state as well as outer conditions continues throughout one's life. Trust in Allah and living the Qur'an and prophetic teachings bring many rewards in the outer state as well as an illumined and guided heart that witnesses Allah's grace and perfect mercy at all times.

Qur'an References: [2:21] [2:45] [39:8] [106:3] [2:260] [3:7] [5:69] [27:92] [47:5] [67:29] [8:2] [11:23]

Will to Realise Unity

The Qur'an describes the earthly human condition as constant strife and turmoil until truth is realised. This natural process of evolvement in consciousness implies departure from the gross and baser level of physical and mental concerns towards the sublime and spiritual. Patience and good expectations are essential disciplines for progress.

The Qur'an describes several historical, personal and collective disasters, natural and man-made, as well as serious mischief and evil acts. Archaeological work and other investigative disciplines have tried to trace the pre-historic origins of human societies and the driving forces that ended up with agricultural settlement and our post-Industrial age. Apart from natural disasters, which were numerous over the life of earth (there have been several major extinctions on earth), the last extinction was that of the dinosaurs. We are now speeding up the sixth extinction through environmental degradations and other human-originated factors. What is it we are all striving for? And how to achieve it?

Only intelligent, reflective human beings will conclude that apart from basic needs for a safe and comfortable shelter, appropriate clothing and good food and health, outer worldly gains, strength and power will only add a small margin to our contentment and happiness. Money and wealth certainly can alleviate outer misery up to a point. Ultimately durable happiness and joy are states of heart that transcend rational and measureable factors.

Our material, mental, intellectual drives and quests lead up to points of connection and unity between diverse and opposing forces in life. All good and bad emanate from the same one source. So do life and death. The mind alone cannot help us with the subtle and transcendental issue of Oneness in creation.

The most durable religious and spiritual paths are maps or instructions that help to have a better feel, taste or understanding of the universal Oneness. This state is not subject to the usual limitations of all thoughts and physical realities. One must leave behind all worldly realities and allow higher consciousness to reveal itself. To experience the presence of the most majestic light of Oneness is the ultimate purpose of human life. It is the source of lasting joy and contentment. The arc of descent from the heavens has now ascended back to its origin. There has only been One – always.

Qur'an References: [2:16] [2:185] [66:73] [26:79] [80:24-32] [18:46] [26:88] [104:3] [57:20] [4:29] [61:11] [2:274] [9:85] [70:24 [2:29]

Knowledge and Ignorance

The human psyche bridges two spheres of consciousness or evolvement: earthly instinct, self-awareness and concern for survival on the one hand, and higher consciousness, moral and spiritual wisdom and knowledge on the other.

Our earthly limitations are equated to darkness while spiritual consciousness of Oneness is equated to light and durable knowledge. Whatever we learn through our senses and mind is only a prelude to higher consciousness with its joyful boundlessness. Thus earthly knowledge is described in the Qur'an as darkness and uncertainty in comparison to the certainty of divine light and its perfection. It is by constant awareness of Allah's attributes and reference to them that we grow in awareness and higher consciousness.

Whenever we refer to Truth or Reality, we imply Allah's higher attributes which we all praise and desire to acquire. When we supplicate to fulfil different needs, we call upon the Bestower of healing, peace, provisions or contentment. Spiritual evolvement takes the faithful and diligent seeker to the shore of reliable inner security through God-consciousness where all His attributes reside. The faithful seeker experiences life and spiritual growth as a delightful journey signposted by Allah's attributes.

The Universe and all of creation praises Allah – the incomparable One. Human beings love and adore or worship Him through His glorious qualities. He is the One Reality that is self-sustaining and envelops the whole universe, which is encompassed within the limitations of space and time. Adam descended from the realm of perfect boundlessness in order to rise again and return to that state of eternal paradise. From that One Cosmic Source, multitudes of qualities and attributes emerged that are like fields of energy that envelop conscious created entities.

God's sacred, unifying light permeates all that is known and unknown and appears at numerous levels of diffusions and fusions. The human soul has had exposure to and knowledge of the original light and is, therefore, sacred. To kill one person unjustly is like murdering all people and to bring life to one person is like giving life to all humanity. All human souls are created with the same potential. Once the lower self is harnessed, then one moves away from the confusion of 'otherness' and instead grows secure in 'Oneness'.

Qur'an References: [23:84] [3:5] [7:180] [17:110] [3:190] [13:02] [14:15] [10:62] [7:56] [39:53] [20:114]

4. WISDOM, GOD-CONSCIOUSNESS & REVELATIONS

Friends of Allah

Adam and Eve complement each other in paradise and on earth. This is both a physical reality and a metaphor of how two different entities emanate from one source and return back to the same unity. A baby begins life mostly concerned with senses and physical gratification. A wise person will be more concerned about meanings in life, insights, subtle knowledge and intuitions – lights of one reality. We all aspire to be in constant awareness of this reality – God.

The well-being of an individual is based upon awareness of intentions and acceptance of responsibility and accountability for actions. A mature person submits to the fact that human needs and desires are endless. Islam – Submission to realities and the real – is followed by faith and trust in God's Perfect Mercy and Justice, irrespective of circumstances. Then one can bask in the security and knowledge of Divine guidance through one's own soul.

The ultimate friends of Allah are the prophets and messengers who have attained their purpose of life, which is to always witness the light of Allah and live according to it. With living faith and trust, the seeker will experience the infinite mercy and grace of God and be in ecstatic gratitude. This is the complete person – a friend of truth.

Human drives are largely based upon fear and concern for what we hold dear or to fulfil desires or needs. Fears and desires are created in the lower levels of consciousness and are the main obstacles to spiritual evolvement. Sorrow, sadness and depression are emotions that relate to the ego or the lower self. Through our intellect, most situations can be understood as natural events, even if undesirable. Awakened beings have the least fears or sorrows; they see events for what they are, without it affecting their hearts. They deal with what can be helped and leave what is beyond human capacity.

Friendship of Allah begins with the love for attributes carried by the soul. With the reduction of egotistic identity, the light of Divine Reality increases until it dominates all realities and shadows. Piety, supplication, remembrance of Allah and all other acts of righteousness and virtues will ultimately lead to total absorption, in perfect contentment, with the glorious Beloved.

Qur'an References: [8:04] [7:26] [13:28] [11:11] [10:64] [3:126] [3:148] [17:19] [10:09-10] [2:03] 4:10] [8:74] [13:28] [3:171] [39:38] [89:27-28] [15:45] [3:41]

Recollection and Awakening

The metaphor of light and darkness signifying illumined 'heavenly' life or dark 'earthly' ignorance is often repeated in the Qur'an. So is the metaphor of being dead while alive. Biological life is only half the story, and awakening to eternal truth is like being fully alive. Those who have this knowledge are equated with 'he who walks in darkness but with a light that shines in front of them while the others are in confused darkness.'

Revealed knowledge, signs, metaphors and examples are there to help us to climb out of earthly darkness to the sacred light that illumines all. This spiritual light is only the outcome of genuine faith and belief, focused intention and good actions, until one enters the zone of connecting the seen and the unseen – mind and heart. The Qur'an asks, is the blind the same as he who has sight? Is darkness and light the same? Is being confused with dualities and multiplicities the same as seeing through the lens of Oneness?

God-consciousness is the advanced stage in the evolution beyond causality and mental limitations. Consciousness has many levels and degrees: the ant is conscious, so is the fox, the baboon and human beings. Each of these is at a different level of awareness. Only human beings can connect with the highest levels of consciousness. The Qur'an says that by faithful commitment to this truth you will come to live a true life that can only be attained through God-consciousness and the realisation that there is no reality except One. The path to this awakening is through pure intentions, dedicated actions and liberation from the lower self. Spiritual righteousness cannot be attained until all love for and attachments to anything other than Allah have vanished. God-consciousness is the gateway to the realm of paradise – here, now and later.

All levels of consciousness emanate from Supreme Consciousness. Early in life we experience personal, conditioned or local consciousness, and then through interaction with others, we expand personal consciousness vertically and horizontally. Biological evolution takes its natural course, whereas spiritual evolvement requires proper intention, willpower and serious application. As we grow in wisdom, knowledge and insights, we find the ocean of consciousness is endless and that local personal consciousness is a barrier to this majestic presence. When the ego-self is extinguished, the original and eternal state of beingness becomes effulgent and clear. Supreme Consciousness is the desired des-

4. WISDOM, GOD-CONSCIOUSNESS & REVELATIONS

tiny for all human beings. Adam fell from the Garden due to self-consciousness and the climb back is through the ladder of the higher self, trust and grace. God-consciousness includes earthly and all other levels of lower consciousness that have emanated from it. The one original Light prevails upon every other light and shadow. Allah is the Light of heavens and earth and once that state is recalled by a being then the journey is complete.

Qur'an References: [3:171] [39:38] [89:27-28] [41:30] [29:41] [2:186] [20:114] [21:35] [7:205] [8:2] [51:55] [80:12] [96:8] [83:21]

Middle People

We are heavenly souls transiting through earth back to heaven. Human life on earth begins with the development of outer and inner senses, then the faculties of imagination, reflection, thinking and higher intellect. Initially a child needs to be helped, protected and guided. The Lord of the universe has endowed parents with lordship for their children. With maturity, greater self-awareness, acceptance of responsibility and inner guidance, the mature person can access inner authority.

The seeker looks for meanings in events and is confident in divine guidance, mercy and forgiveness. A wholesome life implies living fully in the world of dualities and their challenges with constant reference to the soul that brings about stability along the journey. An awakened seeker of truth is in constant reference to the voice and signals of the heart whilst responding to outer stimuli and events. An enlightened person's heart is pure from all attachments and anxieties, for it is illumined by the sacred effulgence of the soul.

Inner freedom is the state of wholesome living. A wholesome life is the harmony of body, mind, heart and soul. Human beings are driven towards improving their physical, material and mental states. The soul is the ever-perfect reference within every person if referred to and followed.

Adam was in the perfect state of paradise. In order to realise the unique gift of his soul, descent to earth took place. On earth we are all driven towards realising perfection at all times and under all circumstances – the state of paradise. This goal is realised when experience of the perfect moment is witnessed at all times, irrespective of our emotions or values. Allah is ever-perfect and so is all that emanates from Him.

The believer trusts in the Divine Presence and governance at all times; therefore, through transformation by worship and God consciousness, one can see the ever-present perfection, irrespective of the event. This is also how the wise and insightful will see grace and order, irrespective of what appears as good or bad. The awakened believer confesses by mind and heart that our earthly journey is sandwiched between the purest of lights and the darkest of states. Indeed we are the middle people, journeying from the most sublime and back to it via the earthly detour.

Qur'an References: [2:143] [3:173] [30:7] [9:111] [6:127] [33:56] [46:13] [33:45-46] [68:52]

4. WISDOM, GOD-CONSCIOUSNESS & REVELATIONS

Perfecting Worship – Deen of Islam

Our earthly life is the training ground for the ascent in consciousness back to the ever-present original Unity. Unless we have done our preparatory work in this life, we will be much handicapped in the realms of the hereafter. If we do not develop spiritual insight and wisdom in this world, we will be like the blind and the dumb in the next.

Worship implies a passion for Allah and willingness to sacrifice everything for the sake of realising Truth. It is also an expression of personal need and inadequacy, and a declaration of hope to reach ultimate contentment and happiness through that love. Acts of worship benefit people according to the extent of their knowledge and understanding of Reality. At the worldly level, acts of worship can soften the heart and egotistic drives as well as enhance ethics and morality.

Proper worship will highlight the importance of accountability in this world whilst being prepared for the hereafter. Through transformative worship we begin to realise Perfect Divine governance, presence and prevalence throughout the universe. It is the path to God-consciousness. The Prophet Muhammad emphasised that an hour of deep reflection or meditation is better than seventy years of formal worship. The quality of life on earth and after death is marked by the quality of the purity at heart, good intentions and appropriate actions.

Every day ends up with its destiny at nightfall and every life reaches its destiny at the point of death. For believers, as well as those who have no interest in spirituality or higher consciousness, there is a desire for a good or happy destiny. In all of our endeavours on earth, our projects, travels and human relationships, we hope for an increased state of contentment and happiness, thereby achieving a better destiny.

Hope is the expectation of a better outcome than the present situation. Sustained wellbeing and happiness may be elusive to most of us on earth yet no one can stop desiring it or striving for it. To realise Divine Perfection and the presence of Allah's glorious attributes and qualities within us is the ultimate gift in life and the source of hope and good expectations, both in the outer world as well as within our heart. Passionate worship will bring this realisation close and ensure its durability.

Qur'an References: [2:173] [3:110] [4:105] [40:60] [41:34] [3:19] [42:13] [2:197] [4:29] [2:188] [3:110] [2:21] [39:8] [53:62] [106:3] [9:111]

Liberating Intentions and Actions

Ease and difficulty, like good and bad, are natural experiences that are unavoidable on earth. We try to reduce what is undesirable and attract what we consider to be good. Human intentions and actions are energised by the interplay of opposites – vices and virtues. We can never exclude difficulties and challenges from our lives, nor can we stop in our attempts to eradicate them. The answer lies in acceptance of the nature of worldly patterns of experience, and then transcendence to higher consciousness through changes in attitude, intentions and appropriate actions.

The gardens we create on earth are like trial runs for the state of the garden in heaven. It is through reflection, meditation, prayer, selfless deeds and patience that we can access the state of inner bliss and happiness at heart – the ever-present paradise within.

The lower self loves ease and comfort, whilst the soul urges the self to submit to it and harmonize with its nature, thus bringing about union with it. Life is in urgent pursuit of its source – the life-giving soul. People of faith and trust in God and in the hereafter are always aware of the possibility that their life may end before attaining the truth. The wise seeker is always self-critical, hard upon his or her own self and lenient with others, always asking forgiveness from the Creator for lack of appropriate intentions and actions. The imperfect being toils towards perfect presence.

With constant remembrance of God and reliance upon His grace in all situations, awareness of the needy self and reference to the soul and its wise authority will result in increasing levels of unison between self and soul. Witnessing that perfection will enhance life's quality. That state of spiritual maturity will lead to spontaneous awareness of our intention, attention and quality of action. Ultimate liberation from all fears and sorrows will be the result of being in the perfect moment at all times.

Qur'an References: [1:7] [3:170] [2:186] [48:2] [3:41] [6:132] [39:38] [89:27-28] [41:30] [21:35] [8:2] [80:12] [6:104] [51:21] [83:21]

CHAPTER FIVE

End of Life and the Universe

- Death and the Hereafter
- Post-Death State
- End of Life on Earth
- Earth, Moon and Planets Disintegrate
- Heavens Collapse: the Cataclysm
- New Life and Consciousness
- Resurrection and Realisation
- What is Truth?
- Hell and Paradise
- Final State – Beingness
- Boundless Oneness – 'Hāhūt'
- Back to Sacred Unity

Death and the Hereafter

All life is contained between two major events: birth and death. These two gateways to the zone of space and time connect our experience of the world with that which is unseen. Birth and death mirror each other and represent a duality that is most important in all of life and consciousness. Immediately after birth we begin to exercise awareness of what is around us and then develop a sense of the self and later on relationships. Most of our life is an exercise of widening and deepening our knowledge and understanding of objectives, events, emotions and other connective factors in life. With maturity our horizons widen and we begin to look at that which is beyond the physical and material domains. The spiritual seeker enjoys reflection, meditation and other transcendental activities that lead to the door of the infinite beyond. Death is a simple transition to that which is beyond our earthly limitations. Deep sleep is a most desirable human need in normal life and death is a permanent version of that.

With the growth of the ego and the idea of selfhood and separation from 'others' we are least concerned about death, except when in mortal danger. The self is a shadow of the soul and always desires to assert itself, its power, strength, durability and other higher qualities. That is why when a person becomes terminally ill we often hear the complaint of 'Why me?' During that time it is not helpful to ask the person who they actually are. For a spiritually evolved person, reality dwells in the soul or the spirit and not in the body or its organs. Like everything else that is alive, one part of us lives on and the other part is left behind. The soul moves on and the body returns to its origin. There are always twos that make up one.

The law of duality carries on in every aspect that we reflect upon. There are two deaths and two births for every person. The first death is a personal death on earth and the second is when everything in the universe will be extinguished. The two births are the biological one that we associate with as our birthday and the hereafter birth on resurrection where everything that ever lived will experience a new life which will reveal everything that had gone before with total clarity. It is curious that respect for the dead has been a common feature with humanity from time immemorial. Even when the person was an utter criminal or a dreadful person there is still a natural tendency to have some respect for the remains of the body. In actual fact, we are paying our respect for the spirit light that has already departed – and not for the decaying body that has been left behind. Death shocks us because it is in this instant that we realise that sacredness has left the body. Whilst the person is alive, however, we are distracted from the respect due to the soul within.

The Prophet Muhammad taught that the hardest three incidents in human life are the moment of death and the presence of the angel of death, the second most shocking period is the second birth or rising from the grave and the third is when facing the light of Allah and the truth of that Reality.

Qur'an References: [3:185] [13:5] [23:99-100] [4:97] [30:19] [30:50] [50:43]

Post-Death State

For thousands of years most humans, nomadic or settled, had some views or ideas regarding life after death. In many agricultural societies, many religious communities would mourn their dead and pray for their ease of transition from life on earth to the hereafter. It was often the norm in Mediterranean civilisations, as well as those in the Americas, to make provisions for the dead person and surround them with what was considered necessary for the journey ahead, including items such as precious materials, personal belongings and food. For thousands of years the tombs of the Pharaohs were raided by robbers because it was widely known that the more important the particular Pharaoh was, the larger the precious hoards left next to him would be. In China, many of the close companions or servants of the Emperor would also be buried with him. The stories and beliefs in the hereafter had been a major part of human culture and education, until pulp fiction replaced it.

Let us consider the model of self-soul polarity in the human make-up. The major and obvious component in this model is the body and its organs including the brain, which is the seat of the mind. At death the soul with its memory of the self and its life on earth will depart, causing a shock to a living system that has now disintegrated. The close relatives and friends will experience sadness and grief for the loss of one of their close ones. It is sometimes said that the soul remains close to the body for a few days and may linger for a week, or visit after forty days or annually. Much depends on the spiritual evolvement of the deceased and the extent of their enlightenment.

Giving birth is a mysterious event that surprises everyone, but usually fills people with some welcome emotions. At death there is a feeling of loss and vacancy. The still living need to be adjusted to the events which are great reminders of the transitory nature of life on earth. On earth we seek what is familiar and whatever provides us with what is perceived as good and conducive for contentment and happiness. The Prophet had said that our life after death would be according to the sum total of our life before death. If we had constantly connected with the Supreme Consciousness that is immortal then the shock is a minor adjustment to your life. Our personal life now joins the infinite ocean of the cosmic soul. The Prophet had said that the grave is part of the garden or a hole in hell.

There are numerous paranormal phenomena that give us ideas regarding the soul's journey and the hereafter. Ghosts and many apparitions are cases where the soul is heavily encumbered by its companion ego on earth. The attachments may have been so tight that the soul is weighed down to remain close by and not carry on towards its destiny. In life after death we are deprived of the ability to act or the will to act as well as to connect or communicate clearly. Our life in the hereafter will be totally energised by the extent and clarity of our attainment of higher (or God-) consciousness on earth.

Qur'an References: [60:13] [40:39] [6:93] [2:25] [16:28]

End of Life on Earth

The Qur'an gives us numerous descriptions of how whatever we consider to be permanent or solid on earth will erupt and disintegrate. Our universe is temporary and whatever exists in it will have a beginning and will have an end. This is the natural cycle within the universe. We are constantly reminded to reflect upon our short life on earth so as to reflect upon the force or the power behind it, within it, before it and after it – Allah.

All that is material on earth will return to its original material state. Solid rocks will become dust. Heavy rocks will float away like clouds. All definable entities, trees, rivers, volcanoes, oceans, ice caps will all disintegrate and lose their boundaries and identity.

We are given numerous examples of how time is relative on earth, and that there is an abode which is not subject to our usual time scales that we shall experience after death. Our human nature demands regular stillness and rest: the need to sleep soundly allows internal adjustment and healing to take place. We are earthly-heavenly at the same time and therefore temporary and eternal. This knowledge is cause for celebration, not sorrow. If we read and see things as they are then we can always be joyful even when personally afflicted with pain or death. Nature is beautiful and the essence and the cause of it is the source of all beauty, which is an attribute of God.

Qur'an References: [11:3] [22:7] [46:3] [35:9] [21:104] [7:25] [36:33] [77:8-11] [99:1-8] [56:1-7]

5. END OF LIFE AND THE UNIVERSE

Earth and Planets Disintegrate

Whenever life appears it will also disappear. Individuals die and so do families, clans and nations. Our planetary system is like a family, with strong links and attachments to each other. Apart from the force of gravity, which is one of the weakest forces in nature but the strongest in terms of planets and stars, there are other forces known and unknown that hold the sky together. Astronomers provide us with dramatic pictures of how stars and planets come to their end after a final great display of fireworks before death. The enormous space that holds the expanding universe is full of unseen activities and balances between strange entities such as matter and anti-matter. Then there are the mysterious black holes which constitute the centres of the galaxies. A black hole is a state where nothing ever can exist and whatever enters it will never leave. This may be a cosmic parable for the hereafter – it simply vanishes with no trace left behind.

Human experiences span a full range from the solid and tangible to the subtlest realities, emotions, thoughts or ideas. We know that energy and matter are totally related and it is due to the four dimensions of time and space that enable us to differentiate them. The table in front of me is temporarily frozen energy in wooden form. After a few years it will disintegrate into its elements and ultimately the subatomic energy from which the atom is born. Our planetary system too will follow its destiny back to its origin of no-thingness – the vast indifferentiable Reality.

Everything in our universe follows patterns and designs which prescribe comings and goings, descent and ascent, as well as weakness and strength, all of which will revert to a point within to the mysterious origin and beginning. The whole universe has emerged from the unseen and will go back to it and much of our human endeavour is driven by the desire to know more of what is unknown. We all seek the ultimate security and knowledge of eternity! The Qur'an reminds us that there are limitations to our search and our efforts, and that as human beings our souls know it all.

Qur'an References: [18:47] [81:128] [54:1] [75:8-10] [84:1-5]

Heavens Collapse – the Cataclysm

Whatever is strong is mirrored by the weakness which accompanies it at all times. The high is mirrored by the low and is inseparable from it. The disintegration of the universe is the mirror image of its emergence, integration and apparent solid foundation and stability.

The end of our universe connects to the beginning of 'new life' or state of awareness. The end of the universe is when whatever had an identity, reality or a sense of life will experience death. Every type of duality that had emerged will now also nullify each other. All small entities, as well as the enormous stars and vast galaxies, will yield to their destiny and return back to the original no-thingness. The cycle of our universe has now come to an end and thus heralds a new beginning, which is of an entirely different nature and occurs in a different zone, a radically different sphere of reality to our space-time box.

Most spiritual practices on earth point towards human transcendence to a state of oblivion, where there is no thought or feeling or any notion of existence – pure consciousness. The state of the vast, incomprehensible no-thingness is there at all times and our universe is a tiny speck hanging on that sacred vastness. The Prophet had said that the earth and the entire heavens are like a small ring perched at the edge of a desert that has no end. This is the relationship of our life on earth to that of truth. A transcendent experience is like a taste of the collapse of one's own heaven. It is the most exhilarating experiences on earth: an epiphany, an experience of nirvana or paradise. If one's inner heaven has not collapsed then we are unlikely to understand the transient nature of our magnificent universe, which is only a sample of the perfect design and pattern behind it. The ultimate prescription for enlightenment is the Prophet's advice, 'Die before you die.'

Qur'an References: [55:37] [55:26] [6:12] [52:9] [70:8] [44:10] [84:1-5] [25:25] [82:1-5]

New Life and Consciousness

The idea of renewal and being given a new lease of life is deep in the human psyche. Every day is in fact like a new lease of life. Some religious people also use the idea of being born again to signify steps in the process of growth in consciousness.

After the universal death and end of all life known or unknown comes a new phase which we describe as heavenly life or the next phase in the hereafter. Everything is reborn but without its shadow, which in the case of the human being is the lower-self or ego. Only souls, spirits and the essential original sacred realities continue without individual will or choice. In this new life there are no shadows, barriers or limitations. On a personal level there is no possibility of deception or excuses. The light of Oneness is effulgent and illumines all. In the Qur'an it is referred to as 'this new earth [that] shines with the light of its Lord.'

All souls and spirits are now free from their previous material encumbrances and are fully alive to this new state. There is no baggage of the past, such as one's wealth, power, or the help of others. There is a sublime clarity and a deep joy of eternal freedom and happiness. There is clear witnessing without any personal ability of power and will to interfere with the witnessed perfection.

This radically new emergence of life is the mirror image of temporary life on earth. It has many of its qualities with regards to awareness or consciousness but none of its shadow plays, dualities, pluralities or oppositions. This new life is far more real and true because it is not subject to the constraints and limitations of time and space and other earthly factors. This new life promises nothing but the truth for all creation. Human beings and other creatures emerge into it in different groups with apprehension, shock and submission. A few are joyful and drift along confidently.

This new emergence of life is the final culmination and natural outcome of life on earth, which has now reached its fullness. The Qur'an describes this event like the blow of a trumpet, announcing the rise of the living from what was considered dead.

Qur'an References: [36:51] [3:30] [2:156] [6:98] [77:8-12] [40:39] [50:15] [12:57] [16:92] [26:88] [54:6-8]

Resurrection and Realisation

The rise of new life is referred to as resurrection. Individuals and nations are gathered in their groups, tribes, nations and similarity of spiritual state. Even animals, birds and other creatures flock together. All of creation experiences a phase of life that was at the essence of their earthly life but dormant and veiled by the ego. The source of our earthly existence is the mysterious gift of life which is a grace from Allah. Now we know the truth, which was partly hidden behind our minds and bodies on earth, that there is only Allah from whose light the world of creation came about, only to evolve and rise back to its original source of Oneness.

The Qur'an describes the new life and resurrection as timeless and true. The dynamics in resurrection include the faint awareness of our previous earthly experience. The Qur'an gives considerable description of the presentation of accounts of what we did on earth. What were our real intentions and the extent of our sincerity, honesty and awareness of the truth within us? How deeply did we reflect upon our nature, God's will and the experience of higher consciousness? Whoever had been on the path of liberation and enlightenment would welcome the account and whoever was not will shun it, for there is no comeback, or personal will or ability to change or improve the difficult situation. Resurrection implies the full unveiling of all shadows and vagueness which earthly life is based upon. The unitive light permeates everything and our earthly deeds are like a distant echo which can barely be remembered.

Whoever welcomes their account and 'balance sheet' takes it willingly with their right hand. But whoever is in doubt or fears their failure (to rise to their spiritual destination) tries to ignore the account or leave it behind them in the same way as we tended to postpone looking at what we did not desire and rushed to meet what was considered pleasurable.

Qur'an References: [39:67] [3:9] [36:51] [50:20] [18:99] [39:68] [78:18] [17:13] [22:56] [56:41-44] [80:38-41] [16:111] [6:38] [39:68]

What is Truth?

In truth, our life on earth could be considered a series of lies with different degrees of the light of truth filtering through – to show the extent of inconsistency. Truth is ever constant and permanent and a lie is a temporary veil that is changeable without any sustainable origin, except for a spark of truth in it. A lie can only exist because it has been given a spark of truth. The less it is a lie the more it has the light of truth, until it becomes absolute truth; and this is the situation after resurrection.

In the hereafter we can read and understand everything as it is in its original format or blueprint. There is utter clarity in all the different patterns and designs which had brought about the universe – truth prevails.

On earth we experience ever-changing and transient realities and seek what we consider 'real' or durable. When we encounter a person we first see their shape and hear their voice and maybe later we understand their inner intention and condition of heart. In the hereafter the situation is reversed. The first experience is that of the innermost and original design and we may also see the colour or the vague shadow of the earthly 'personality'. Whatever there was in the past on earth may appear as a vague shadow. The nature of divine Light now prevails and shows everything as it is in 'reality'.

It is the original sacred Light (Allah is the Light of the heavens and the earth and to Him belongs all) that prevails totally in the hereafter. It is through God's Light that everything is ever understood and known, and there is no possibility or allowance for personal interference in the hereafter as was the case on earth.

Human life on earth is a phase in between two unknowns: one is the unknown before birth and the other is after death. Our life on earth is like a nursery which enables us to plug into higher consciousness and enjoy the regular reference to it, in order to see through realities as they really are. Now everything shows itself as it really is. There are no veneers, camouflages or deceptions. The nursery on earth allowed us to play some of these tricks which are a part of nature. Here nature has reverted to its heavenly origin – clear light and perfected delight.

Qur'an References: [3:152] [25:15] [79:36-41] [17:99] [55:26-27] [96:8] [75:22] [42:7] [6:2]

Hell and Paradise

Our life on earth has taught us love for ease, comfort and well-beingness. All of our actions are balanced between attracting what we desire and repulsing or turning away from that which is not desirable. When an affliction or a difficult situation becomes too intense we call it 'hell' and when a joyful state opens hearts and spreads happiness we call it 'paradise'. Our earthly experience had given us samples of all the possibilities that exist in the seen and the unseen. We have clear preferences for joy and happiness, unless our psyche, mind and heart are so disturbed that we no longer are able to differentiate and are completely confused. In the hereafter, where time has ceased, hell and paradise take on what appears to be a permanent nature. Thus they are labelled as eternal.

From before formal religions, humankind had imagined hell and paradise in the heavens. And most human endeavours on earth were in preparation for the return to paradise. The Qur'an describes the rise of Adam and his consciousness as taking place in paradise. It is for that reason that all human beings long to be in the paradisiacal state. The Qur'an and the prophetic teachings describe the presence of paradise as being there at all times and that it is not a 'place'. Paradise is described as being wider than the heavens and earth. It is a state of constant and perfect joy and happiness. This state of permanency can be imagined as simply being frozen in time. When an event or situation gives us joy on earth we like to freeze it in a photograph, in order to remember it more often. It may be that we are even genetically programmed to desire paradise and fear hell.

People in hell are in a state of constant turmoil as there is no stability, even in the normal fire. It is a state of perpetual agitation and endless disintegration, whereas that of paradise is of perpetual perfect presence. People in hell have some vague memory of the past. As for people in paradise, some of them even ask for a higher level of light now that they have seen the prevailing divine light shining upon all. The Qur'an says that they say they have experienced the joys of paradise before (on earth) and they ask their Lord to go beyond all aspects of experiences to the eternal light, which is absolute and beyond description.

Qur'an References: [69:25-36] [2:39] [54:48] [10:9] [84:10-15] [77:42] [2:201] [30:16] [2:221] [26:90] [3:133]

5. END OF LIFE AND THE UNIVERSE

Final State – Beingness

Whatever we liked or desired on earth we wanted to last forever: contentment, wellbeing, joy and happiness. We desired a good relationship to be eternal. We aspired for well-beingness and on-goingness. These states are all shadows or reflections of the truth of the final state which is infinite and was there at the very beginning. Creation began from absolute perfection and will end up there. Adam in paradise was in that state to begin with, but an aspect of his consciousness arose (referred to as a whisper of Satan) wanting to know eternity. Thus he descended to earth to experience its temporary nature and thereby cry genuinely for eternity. A baby knows more about what it does not want as it spits out what it doesn't like in its mouth. We too know more of what we do not want – often that which is unfamiliar and does not connect with past experiences. What we always want and desire is eternal goodness and paradise. In this final cycle of experience we go past all changes, interactions and dualities, and come close to singularity.

In religions it is often referred to as returning to God's abode or the mansion of the Lord. Even Jerusalem can be an understandable label. There are no disturbances if one is in the state of the garden. In hell there is a constant disintegration. This is the final state in the unseen to which we return and it resembles and/or mirrors the state from where we emerged in the first place on earth. There is still some personal consciousness or experience before it gets fully submerged in pure consciousness or 'Lāhūt'.

Qur'an References: [10:56] [56:41-49] [31:28] [2:281] [14:48] [17:13-14] [69:19] [41:20-23] [69:19-25] [71:17-18] [49:44]

Boundless Oneness – 'Hahut'

The most joyful state on earth is not describable, for it occurs when thoughts cease and all conscious awareness stops. It is adrift at the edge of space and time. We describe wonderful experiences as 'mindboggling' or 'unbelievable' or even as madness. These are human expressions trying to describe the inexpressible or boundless Oneness. Divine Oneness is not subject to any of our human understanding or limitations for it is the beginning of all beginnings and the light of all lights. Indeed, physical light and photons emerge from this mysterious sacred light and return to it. Life on earth is dependent upon the energy of visible light and heat.

Life on earth goes through cycles and phases at numerous levels: biological, psychological, mental, emotional and spiritual, ending up with the unity between self and soul, and the return to their original abode after passing through death. At the end, all of the turmoils of the collapse of the universe, resurrection, purifications and experiences of hell and paradise, all go back to boundless Oneness. The curtain is now almost drawn.

The Prophet was asked where Satan would end up and he answered that at the end all is forgiven and returns back to Allah. This is the stage of absolute no-thingness, Singularity before any dualities. At the source of the Light of lights there are no distinctions whatsoever; simply pure Essence or one and only One. The Qur'an has numerous reminders to human beings that most of the activities on earth and human turmoil are exercises for the intellect and heart; for discriminating people to refer back to the source (Allah) for guidance. The Qur'an says that no human being is spared difficulties or afflictions on earth so that they may ponder the most important question as to the origin of all these challenges and the way to respond appropriately. Allah is the original Cause and to that Essence all will return. With clarity in mind and purity of heart, good intentions and actions, the enlightened human being is always energised and guided by the divine Presence.

Qur'an References: [11:4] [17:99] [36:78-79] [6:73] [36:81-83] [29:20] [20:55] [22:5-6] [41:39] [6:94] [112:1-2]

5. END OF LIFE AND THE UNIVERSE

Back to Sacred Unity

Allah is described in the Qur'an as being the light of the heavens and earth, the ever-living, the ever-knowing and perfect eternal Governor of whatever is in the heavens and earth. The whole universe is an emanation of His mercy and love. Everything known and unknown is energised by that original power – unfathomable, beyond our ability to comprehend, understand or define. However, the human soul which is within the metaphoric heart carries an imprint of that reality and its qualities. It is through that inner connection that we will come to know the universal Presence of Allah beyond belief or human thought. A fortunate seeker of spirituality will come to know that in truth there is only that Light and everything else is a trace or shadow of it.

Our universe may be one of numerous multi-verses that already exist but are separated by mysterious barriers between them. At the beginning of life there was only the Light of Allah. During life on earth there was also the same light that permeated and sustained it. During our human life on earth the sacred light filtered through the divine qualities and attributes (Allah's names). Now that the whole universe had returned to its origin there remains the absolute unique Oneness, whose subtle lights and forces hold the universe and all creations within it together. Now everything is back at rest from where it emerged. In truth nothing is gained and nothing lost. Utter perfection reigns as it has always been in truth.

Personal and universal death announces a most majestic conclusion to a beautiful and glorious creation, reflecting the eternal truth of the supreme Presence of the one Creator and Master of all – Allah. When followed with unconditional faith and proper understanding, the Qur'an can provide prescriptions and guidance that will bring about liberation from the illusion of otherness and the realisation of the ever-present Oneness. Thus, 'Whoever follows my [Allah's] guidance there will be no fear upon them nor will they grieve'.

Qur'an References: [99:4-5] [30:11] [75:12] [24:35] [21:104] [2:38]

Glossary

FTR: FaTaRa, to crack open, rend asunder, tear apart; come forth, originate, create. Related: fitrah: Man's natural disposition, his innate nature, the human blueprint, the natural constitution with which a child is created in the mother's womb. Related verbs: aftara to break fast; infatara to become, cracked open (82:1). Derivatives: futūr, fissure; fatūr, breakfast; iftār, breaking of fast at sunset; infitār, cleaving asunder.

Hāhūt: Boundless, Essential Oneness of God. Derived from the Divine Name Huwa, "He," and formed by analogy with the following terms, here given in descending hierarchical order: Lāhūt : the Divine (creative) Nature; Jabarūt : the Divine Power or Immensity, the world beyond form; Malakūt : the Kingdom of the angels, the spiritual world; Nāsūt (or Mulk): human nature, and in particular man's bodily form.

HWA: Vain or egotistical desire; passions; impulsiveness; from hawa to fall down; hawiya to love, desire.

Ihsān: Virtuous conduct; Performance of good deeds, excellence, beneficence. The culmination of the progression from islām (qv.) to īmān (qv.) to the state of "though one does not see Allah one acts in full certainty that He sees oneself". From ahsana, to act well, pleasingly, expertly, to do good; hasuna to be or become handsome, beautiful, good, to be in a desirable condition. Derivatives: husn, beauty; muhsin, person in state of ihsān, beneficent, charitable.

Īmān: Faith, trust, belief, acceptance. From amana to believe and amina, to be tranquil in heart and mind, to become safe or secure, to trust; āmana to render secure, grant safety. Īmān is being true to the trust with respect to which Allah has confided in one by a firm, believing of the heart, not by professing it on the tongue only.

Islām   Submission to the Divine patterning and decree. From aslama to submit, commit (oneself); salama, to be safe and sound, unimpaired, intact, blameless, to be free; sallama to preserve, to deliver, hand over, salute. The Muslim is he who trusts in and submits to Allah. Islam comes before full faith and certainty can take root, i.e. īmān (qv.), which then transforms the active state of the slave into that of ihsān (qv.).

Jabarūt   The invisible realm of potentialities, the world of Divine Omnipotence or Immensity. Generally considered by metaphysicists to be the highest of the three worlds (Mulk, Malakut).

Khalifah   Steward, guardian, representative, successor. From Khalafa: to be behind, come after.

Lāhūt   The Realm of Divine Nature. Opposed to Nāsūt (human nature). Ibn 'Arabī says that an-Nāsūt is like a form or container of which al-Lāhūt is the content, or the secret life. Lāhūt is derived from ilāh, "divinity," nāsūt from insān, "man."

Malakūt   The Invisible, celestial world: 'alim al-ghayb; the realm of angels and spirits.

Mulk   Also referred to as Nāsūt, The worldly dominion, the Seen, the realm of sensory perception, human nature.

NWR   NaWaRa To illuminate. Related: nār, fire; nūr, light.

Rūh   Spirit, soul, breath of life (pl. arwāh). From raha, to do anything in the evening or at sunset, to go away, and rawwaha to refresh, animate. Rūh is spirit, which is subtle, while nafs is self, which is rigid.

Taqwā   God-consciousness; precautious, fearful awareness of (obedience to) Allah; devoutness. From waqā to guard, to preserve, shield, prevent (a danger); and ittaqā to beware, be on one's guard, protect oneself.

About the Author

SHAYKH FADHLALLA HAERI was born in Karbala, Iraq, a descendant of several generations of well-known and revered spiritual leaders. Educated in Europe and America. He founded a number of companies in the Middle East and worked as a consultant in the oil industry. He travelled extensively on a spiritual quest, which led to his eventual rediscovery of the pure and original Islamic heritage of his birth.

His main work has been to make traditional Islamic teachings more comprehensible and widely available to the modern seeker through courses and publications.

Shaykh Fadhlalla Haeri is currently engaged in lecturing and writing books and commentaries on the Holy Qur'an and related subjects, with particular emphasis on ethics, self-development and gnosis ('irfan).

He is now based in South Africa where he established the Academy of Self Knowledge: http://www.askonline.co.za

The eBook versions of all the following books can be accessed and purchased through the above website's eBooks Portal section which then offers links to quick purchase and download options for dedicated Kindle, Kobo and Nook eReaders, Apple iOS devices, as well as Kindle, Kobo and Nook apps for Windows PC's, Macs, smart phones and tablets.

Hard copies can be purchased through Amazon or by contacting us at zp@askonline.co.za

Zahra Publications eBooks Portal Web Address:
http://www.askonline.co.za/ebooks.php

General Books on Islam

Living Islam – East and West

Ageless and universal wisdom set against the backdrop of a changing world: application of this knowledge to one's own life is most appropriate.

The Elements of Islam/Thoughtful Guide to Islam

An introduction to Islam through an overview of the universality and light of the prophetic message.

The Qur'an & Its Teachings

Beams of Illumination from the Divine Revelations

A collection of teachings and talks with the objective of exploring deeper meanings of Qur'anic Revelations.

Commentary on Four Selected Chapters of the Qur'an

The Shaykh uncovers inner meanings, roots and subtleties of the Qur'anic arabic terminology.

The Cow: Commentary on Chapters One and Two of the Holy Qur'an

The first two chapters of the Qur'an give guidance regarding inner and outer struggle. Emphasis is on understanding key Qur'anic terms.

The Family of Imran

This book is a commentary on the third chapter of the Qur'an, the family of 'Imran which includes the story of Mary, mother of 'Isa (Jesus).

The Essential Message of the Qur'an

Teachings from the Qur'an such as purpose of creation, Attributes of the Creator, nature of human beings, decrees governing the laws of the universe, life and death.

Heart of Qur'an and Perfect Mizan

Commentary on chapter Yasin. This is traditionally read over the dead person: if we want to know the meaning of life, we have to learn about death.

Journey of the Universe as Expounded in the Qur'an

The Qur'an traces the journey of all creation, seeing the physical, biological and geological voyage of life as paralleled by the inner spiritual evolution of wo/man.

The Qur'anic Prescription for Life

Understanding of the Qur'an is made accessible with easy reference to key issues concerning life, and the path of Islam.

Sufism & Islamic Psychology and Philosophy

Beginning's End

This is a contemporary outlook on sufi sciences of self knowledge, exposing the challenge of our modern lifestyle that is out of balance.

Cosmology of the Self

Islamic teachings of Tawheed (Unity) with insights into the human self: understanding the inner landscape is essential foundation for progress on the path of knowledge.

Decree and Destiny

A lucid exposition of the extensive body of Islamic thought on the issue of free will and determinism.

The Elements of Sufism/Thoughtful Guide to Sufism

Sufism is the heart of Islam. This introduction describes its origins, practices, historical background and its spread throughout the world.

Happiness in Life and After Death – An Islamic Sufi View

This book offers revelations and spiritual teachings that map a basic path towards wholesome living without forgetting death: cultivating a constant awareness of one's dual nature.

The Journey of the Self

After introducing the basic model of the self, there follows a simple yet complete outline of the self's emergence, development, sustenance, and growth toward its highest potential.

Leaves from a Sufi Journal

A unique collection of articles presenting an outstanding introduction to the areas of Sufism and original Islamic teachings.

The Sufi Way to Self-Unfoldment

Unfolding inner meanings of the islamic ritual practices towards the intended ultimate purpose to live a life honorable and fearless, with no darkness, ignorance or abuse.

Witnessing Perfection

Delves into the universal question of Deity and the purpose of life. Durable contentment is a result of 'perfected vision'.

Practices & Teachings of Islam

Calling Allah by His Most Beautiful Names

Attributes or Qualities resonate from their Majestic and Beautiful Higher Realm into the heart of the active seeker, and through it back into the world.

Fasting in Islam

This is a comprehensive guide to fasting in all its aspects, with a description of fasting in different faith traditions, its spiritual benefits, rules and regulations.

The Inner Meanings of Worship in Islam – A Personal Selection of Guidance for the Wayfarer

Here is guidance for those who journey along this path, from the Qur`an, the Prophet's traditions, narrations from the Ahl al-Bayt, and seminal works from among the Ahl al-Tasawwuf of all schools of thought.

The Pilgrimage of Islam

This is a specialised book on spiritual journeying, offering the sincere seeker keys to inner transformation.

Prophetic Traditions in Islam – On the Authority of the Family of the Prophet

Offers a comprehensive selection of Islamic teachings arranged according to topics dealing with belief and worship, moral, social and spiritual values.

The Wisdom (Hikam) of Ibn Ata'allah – Translation and Commentary

These aphorisms of Ibn Ata'Allah, a Shadili Shaykh, reveal the breadth and depth of an enlightened being who reflects divine unity and inner transformation through worship.

The Sayings and Wisdom of Imam Ali

A selection of this great man's sayings gathered together from authentic and reliable sources. They have been carefully translated into modern English.

Talks & Courses

Ask Course 1 – The Sufi Map of the Self

This workbook explores the entire cosmology of the self through time, and maps the evolution of the self from before birth through life, death and beyond.

Ask Course 2 – The Prophetic Way of Life
This workbook explores how the code of ethics that govern religious practice and the Prophetic ways are in fact transformational tools to enlightened awakening.

Friday Discourses – Volume 1
The Shaykh addresses many topics that influence Muslims at the core of what it means to be a Muslim in today's global village.

Songs of Iman on the Roads of Pakistan
A series of talks given on the divergence between 'faith' and 'unbelief' during a tour of the country in 1982 which becomes a reflection of the condition occurring in the rest of the world today.

Poetry & Aphorisms

Sound Waves
A collection of aphorisms that help us reflect and discover the intricate connection between self and soul.

Beyond Windows
Offering moving and profound insights of compassion and spirituality through these anthologies of connections between slave self and Eternal Lord.

101 Helpful Illusions
Everything in creation has a purpose relevant to ultimate spiritual Truth. This book highlights natural veils to be transcended by disciplined courage, wisdom and insight.

Bursts of Silence
Inspired aphorisms provide keys to doors of inner knowledge, as well as antidotes to distraction and confusion.

Ripples of Light

Inspired aphorisms which become remedies for hearts that seek the truth.

Pointers to Presence

A collection of aphorisms providing insights into consciousness and are pointers to spiritual awakening.

Autobiography

Son of Karbala

The atmosphere of an Iraq in transition is brought to life and used as a backdrop for the Shaykh's own personal quest for self-discovery and spiritual truth.

www.ingramcontent.com/pod-product-compliance
Lightning Source LLC
Chambersburg PA
CBHW060200050426
42446CB00013B/2920